Trump Effect

Professor Karina V. Korostelina presents insights into the "Trump effect" and explains how the support for Trump among the American general public is based on three complementary pillars. First, Trump champions a specific conception of American national identity that empowers his supporters. Second, Trump's leadership has, to an extent, been crafted from his ability to recognize where and with whom he can get the most return on his investment (e.g. his political comments) and address the perceived general malaise in the U.S. Trump also mirrors the emotions of a disenfranchised American public and inspires the use of frustration-based anger and insults to achieve desired aims. He addresses the public's intolerance of uncertainty and ambivalence by providing simpler solutions to complex national problems and by blurring the boundary between the leading political parties. Further, Trump employs existing political polarization and has established a new kind of morality. Third, Trump challenges the existing political balance of power within the U.S. and globally.

The overarching goal of this book is to show how the popularity of Trump has revealed substantial problems in the social, political, and economic fabric of American life.

Aimed at the general public and students in the U.S. and internationally, the book goes beyond many explanations of the "Trump effect." Using a multidisciplinary theoretical lens, it provides a systemic multifaceted analysis based on multiple theories of social identity, emotions, cognitions, morality, and power to explain the broader social phenomena of the rise of individuals in society.

Karina V. Korostelina is a Professor at the School for Conflict Analysis and Resolution, and a Director of the Program on History, Memory, and Conflict at George Mason University. Professor Korostelina is a social psychologist whose work focuses on social identity and identity-based conflicts, intergroup insult, the nation building processes, role of history in conflict and post-conflict societies, conflict resolution, and peacebuilding. She is a recipient of thirty-nine fellowships and grants. She has edited six books and authored nine books and numerous articles.

Trump Effect

Karina V. Korostelina

LONDON AND NEW YORK

First published 2017 by Routledge

2 Park Square, Milton Park, Abingdon, Oxfordshire OX14 4RN

52 Vanderbilt Avenue, New York, NY 10017

Routledge is an imprint of the Taylor & Francis Group, an informa business

First issued in paperback 2019

Library of Congress Cataloging-in-Publication Data
Names: Korostelina, K. V. (Karina Valentinovna) author.
Title: Trump effect / Karina V. Korostelina.
Description: Milton Park, Abingdon, Oxon ; New York, NY :
    Routledge, 2017. | Includes bibliographical references and index.
Identifiers: LCCN 2016033938 | ISBN 9781138281462 (hbk) |
    ISBN 9781315271170 (ebk)
Subjects: LCSH: Trump, Donald, 1946– | Presidents—United States—
    Election—2016. | Presidential candidates—United States. | Political
    culture—United States. | United States—Politics and government—2009–
Classification: LCC E901.1.T78 K67 2017 | DDC 973.932092—dc23
LC record available at https://lccn.loc.gov/2016033938

ISBN: 978-1-138-28146-2 (hbk)
ISBN: 978-0-367-88563-2 (pbk)

Typeset in Times New Roman
by Apex CoVantage, LLC

To Charles, my husband and best friend, a partner in intellectual endeavors, and a fellow world explorer.

Contents

Acknowledgments

I want to express my gratitude to all my colleagues who supported me in this endeavor, especially to Sandra Cheldelin, Leila Dane, Daniel Rothbart, and Mara Schoeny. Special thanks to Kevin Avruch, the Dean of my home institution, the School of Conflict Analysis and Resolution, George Mason University, for creating the encouraging environment of creativity. The help of my graduate assistant, Laura Collins, was essential for the success of this project.

I am very thankful to my three reviewers whose detailed comments helped shape the book. I offer special thanks to Natalja Mortensen, senior editor at Routledge, for her support, professionalism, and efficiency at various stages of this work.

I also express my deepest gratitude to my husband, Charles, who inspired and supported me in writing this book and provided numerous invaluable insights and comments. I am very thankful to my daughter, Olivia, for her suggestions at the last stages of the writing. Discussions and conversations with them were the best part of this project.

Introduction

People are largely united in their pursuit to make their communities, nations, and the world a better place. They are, however, often sharply divided over which beliefs and actions are needed to achieve it. In this pursuit, people adopt a set of beliefs and ideas that represent their own reality in the most satisfying way. This perception of the world typically represents the values they have developed over time and helps them explain current affairs and predict the future. People construct their version of reality based on several selected facts and certain interpretations. They purposefully choose to stress some matters while completely undermining other values, and they prefer to adopt some explanations of current events rather than others. People make these constructed realities meaningful for themselves through interaction with others, helping to crystalize their own beliefs into the facts and norms they use in their everyday social communication. These created realities then function as a framework defining people's behavior. As a result, people follow particular authority figures while entirely mistrusting others.[1]

People act based on their understanding of circumstances, on their beliefs of what is true, and, thus, make decisions based on their perception rather than on the full spectrum view of any given situation.[2] People create conflicts with others because of their tendency to construct a sometimes completely opposite interpretation of the same situation. They also defend themselves from perceived threats and fight with rivals based on negative characteristics that have been attributed to these rivals. For example, unemployment is an objective reality, but people create different explanations for who is to blame for this reality: Is it immigrants who are taking their jobs, employers who promote minorities based on affirmative action, or corporations that ship jobs to foreign countries? Depending on their view, people will tend to unite with the particular group that affirms their perceptions, supporting this group and the specific rules governing group behavior. It is less important for them that the full picture of a situation may not support their perceptions. Rather, what is vital is the specific version of reality they believe in.

Political reality is no different. For voters, it is less important what social and economic data point to regarding the current situation of the country. They usually do not have knowledge about this data or even the structures of political institutions or each candidate's platform.³ The most crucial factors for them are how they construct their reality and what they personally experience and believe in. Depending on these views, people may support a particular political party yet engage with and support a specific candidate of a different party.

Donald Trump understands this well. As a successful real estate developer, he subscribes to the view that perception is everything—perception is reality. For example, people tend to choose a particular house they purchase based on their own self-perception, and, thus, it is crucial that they create the best impression of themselves and their lives. As a real estate investor, Trump also understands that people buy and sell based on their opinions of the market. As Trump has stated about his own business, "My net worth fluctuates and it goes up and down with markets and with attitudes and with feelings. Even my own feelings."⁴ In the *Art of the Deal*, Trump explains that the best road to success is not being successful but portraying oneself as successful. He refers to it as "bravado." "The final key to the way I promote is bravado. I play to people's fantasies. People may not always think big themselves, but they can still get very excited by those who do. That's why a little hyperbole never hurts. People want to believe that something is the biggest and the greatest and the most spectacular."⁵

This book aims to explain how the perceptions of the American public have not only led to Trump's rise as a U.S. presidential candidate and the Republican nominee. The book shows how Trump has created a new political value system by championing people's perceptions and demonstrating that previously questioned ways of expressing frustration and anger are, in fact, acceptable. Further, this book demonstrates how Trump has built on people's fears and grievances by mirroring their emotions and supporting their opinions and interpretations of a myriad of socio-political and economic issues.

In comparison with other publications that emphasize certain factors, this book posits that the "Trump effect" is a more complex phenomenon based on three complementary pillars. First, Trump champions a specific conception of American national identity that empowers his supporters. Trump's leadership has, to an extent, been crafted from his ability to recognize where and with whom he can get the most return on his investment (e.g. his political comments) and address the perceived general malaise in the U.S. Moreover, Trump not only mirrors the emotions of the American public but also inspires the use of frustration-based anger and insults to achieve desired aims. He addresses the public's intolerance of uncertainty and ambivalence by providing simpler solutions and blurring the boundary between the leading political parties. Further, Trump employs existing political polarization and has established a new kind of morality. Third, Trump is both challenging the existing political balance of power and promoting coercion and dominance within the U.S. and globally.

The overarching aim of this book is to show how the popularity of Trump has revealed substantial problems in the social, political, and economic fabric of American life. Despite many publications linking Trump to low-educated, blue-collar workers, statistics show his support, in fact, crosses demographic lines—education, income, age, political party, and religious affiliation.[6] Many of these voters believe increasing globalization is undermining the national interests of the U.S. and the established concept of American citizenship.

The rise of populist parties across Europe and the British vote to leave the European Union underscores the reality that there exists a strong demand within some segments of these populations for fundamental socio-political change, which has at its core a restoration of each respective country's greatness by reestablishing national control and protection of borders, culture and national identity, and the promotion of the interests and positions of their native citizens.

First, support for Trump is connected with deindustrialization, depression, and a rising sense of economic misery. A major concern of many voters concerns the destructive free trade deals that have driven many jobs out of the U.S. and into other countries, causing the deindustrialization of America and economic despair among White blue-collar workers. The falling demand for industrial labor has led to a decline in prime-age male employment that decreased from 98 percent in 1954 to 88 percent today.[7] Voters who believe their government should protect their nation from the pitfalls of the global economy are driven by such economic distress to vote for Trump. Moreover, there is a strong correlation between support for Trump and the rise of the middle-aged White death rate resulting from drug and alcohol abuse, and other related health problems.[8] The results of interviews conducted by Working America of sixteen hundred White working-class voters showed "people are fed up, people are hurting, they are very distressed about the fact that their kids don't have a future . . . People are much more frightened than they are bigoted."[9]

Second, many members of the White population in the U.S. are exhibiting feelings of cultural stress resulting from growing illegal immigration, perceived resistance to assimilation, and worsening race relations.[10] Eighty percent of Trump supporters believe that immigration is a burden that causes more problems than benefits for their country.[11] They feel that their way of life is changing at a pace they are not able to comprehend or accept. They are unable to understand why people who come to the U.S. illegally have access to government protection and social benefits. They believe their jobs are not only disappearing due to outsourcing aboard but are also being taken by newcomers. They are, thus, demanding immediate protection from the growing influx of immigrants. Similarly, the vote to leave the EU in Great Britain was partially caused by the negative reaction to the arrival of 630,000 foreign nationals in 2015 alone.[12]

Third, the Trump campaign addresses the fears of the American population that have resulted from the inability of Western elites to handle the wars and humanitarian crises in the Middle East and to contain the threat and expansion of Islamic extremism. In order to quell their fears and dampen their anxieties, 44 percent of Americans "seek out a strongman leader who would preserve a status quo they feel is under threat and impose order on a world they perceive as increasingly alien."[13] Sixty-five percent of them support the Republican Party. These voters tend to believe that most threats originate from outside of the U.S., such as the threat of ISIS, Russia, or Iran, and want "to use government power to eliminate the threats."[14]

Finally, Trump's rise is rooted in a growing mistrust of government among the American population. Only 40 percent of low-income members of the population have trust in American political elites[15] and just 19 percent say they can trust the government always or most of the time.[16] Among Republicans, only 13 percent have trust in government and 75 percent of Republicans believe that the government needs major reform, a significant increase from 43 percent in 1997.[17] Republicans and Republican-leaning independents who are angry with government see Trump as the most favorable candidate.[18] They believe he can change the way the government operates, in addition to promoting a complete and necessary overhaul of the political leadership.

These grievances, which are held by significant parts of the American population, have not been taken into account by many within the U.S. political establishment, including the executive branch leadership. Rather, the current administration has sought to continue promoting a globalized economy, expand immigration and an open border policy. The policies in place have provided little opportunity for these large segments of society to receive the benefits of globalization. High levels of socioeconomic inequality and low upward mobility have made them feel desperate and uneasy about their children's future. Moreover, their interests have not been fully addressed and little empathy has been given to their real concerns. Instead, the voices of those in economic misery and experiencing cultural stress have been labeled as ignorant, bigoted, and prejudiced. The concept of a shared society has not evolved as desired.

The analysis presented in this book will be based on the triangulation of several methods: an analysis of speeches and postings made by Mr. Trump; an analysis of polls and published interviews with his supporters; and an analysis of available reports, opinion articles, and academic research on the drivers behind Trump's popular support. The methods of data analysis include thematic analysis, critical discourse analysis, and content analysis.

Chapter 1, "Candidate Trump," discusses the overarching problems globalization has brought to Western countries in both the U.S. and throughout Europe, as well as specific issues that characterize economic, social, and political life in the U.S. during the 2016 campaign. This chapter compares the different styles of the leading U.S. presidential candidates, Hilary Clinton and Donald Trump, and their approaches to major problems facing the U.S. and the world. In order to better understand the Trump effect, the chapter further explores if Trump's actions are "natural," based on his instinctive reactions to issues in American society, or "professional," based on his business skills and knowledge, which allows him to instrumentally manipulate desires and respond to the needs of his followers.

Chapter 2, "Win with Me," discusses how Trump has created and champions a particular social identity for his supporters and how people connect to the narratives he produces. He provides people with a particular meaning of national identity and defines the boundaries of groups, their legitimacy and positions within the nation. The chapter provides a detailed analysis of how Trump has created a strong narrative that empowers specific groups within the American society, which, in turn, increases their hopes and self-esteem. Through acquiring this new identity shared with Trump, people connect themselves with the very idea of winning and, thereafter, position themselves as victors. Trump also inspires their willingness to put down other groups and even support intergroup hostility.

Chapter 3, "The Great Insulter," describes the instruments Trump uses to create an empowering identity, including favorable comparison and exclusion, insults, and bullying. Trump employs social insults to prove he is better than others, to justify this behavior by blaming others for provoking it, to distance himself from others, to strip people of some privileges, to present himself as more powerful, and to emphasize his higher validity and social weight in comparison with others. These insults serve as a mechanism of connection and identification. People "feed" on Trump's insults to his and their adversaries to achieve similar feelings of high self-esteem and power. His supporters are also empowered by connecting to and approving of Trump's bullying behavior. For Trump's supporters, the ability to talk mean to others and the "power to insult" others are connected with the perception of having a higher status within the social hierarchy.

Chapter 4, "Angry as Hell," shows how Trump displays the same emotions as his supporters and how this, in turn, deeply connects him with his supporters and any newcomers who share these same emotions. This has the effect of providing a feeling of unity. The chapter analyses how Trump employs displaced, retaliatory, and instrumental aggression. As frustration causes pain and discent, anger and aggression emerge as an inevitable part of behavior and strongly connects Trump to his supporters. Trump also employs perceptions of threats among American people and reinforces the perception among his supporters that they have increasingly fewer rights, resources, and power in comparison with other ethnic or racial groups; in comparison with their previous position in American society; and in comparison with their expectations. To address these feelings, he has promoted the idea of denial of certain rights enjoyed by outgroups and emphasized the legitimate position of his supporters, their exclusive right to control the country, make decisions, and define policies. The chapter also shows how Trump supporters mirror his bravado and have acquired a sense of self-importance and a feeling of empowerment as a result.

Chapter 5, "The World Is Simple," discusses how Trump helps to reduce the anxiety and frustration of his supporters by simplifying their perception of the world. His supporters "feed" on the simplifications Trump produces through stereotypes and labeling, and they feel more confident in their understanding of the world. To reduce uncertainties and ambiguity and provide closure to his supporters, Trump has sought to formulate simple resolutions of entrenched problems. In addition, Trump addresses political ambivalence by deviating from established party lines that may positively resonate with his supporters, and provides them with a higher degree of cognitive certainty and liberation.

Chapter 6, "The Good, the Bad, and the Ugly," describes how Trump has provided his supporters with a value system clear of moral dilemmas and "political correctness" by employing dualistic perceptions and dividing the world into winners and losers, evil and good, laborers and parasites. Trump also addresses the direct needs of his supporters at the expense of other people and groups and encourages their desire to control the behavior of others.

Chapter 7, "Making America Great Again," discusses how Trump has used dissatisfaction with collaborative concept of power as connected with weakness and failings. He has associated this power with existing politicians and has positioned himself as anti-establishment. Moreover, Trump has been promoting an idea of power as a zero-sum game that is coercive and dominant and has promised to make America great by changing the political power balance and reducing the perceived illegitimate access certain groups and countries have to resources.

The conclusion addresses the implication of the "Trump effect" for the election and American society as a whole.

Notes

1. Adams, Tony. E. "Speaking for others: Finding the "whos" of discourse." *Soundings: An Interdisciplinary Journal* 88, no. 3/4 (2005): 331–345; Gergen, Kenneth. J., *The Saturated Self, Dilemmas of Identity in Contemporary Life*. New York: Basic Books. 2nd ed, 2001.

2. Goffman, Erving. *The Presentation of Self in Everyday Life.* New York: Anchor, 1959; Raskin, Jonathan D. "Constructivism in psychology: Personal construct psychology, radical constructivism, and social constructionism." *American Communication Journal,* 5, no. 3 (2002).

3. Somin, Ilya. *Democracy and Political Ignorance: Why Smaller Government Is Smarter.* Standford, CA: Stanford University Press, 2013.

4. Lappin, Joan. "It's Not Reality but Perception That Counts," *Forbes,* May 22, 2009. accessed May 29, 2016, http://www.forbes.com/2009/05/22/target-tiffany-recession-personal-finance-investing-ideas-donald-trump.html

5. Trump, Donald. J. *Trump: The Art of the Deal.* New York, NY: Ballantine Books, 2005.

6. Taub, Amanda. "The Rise of American Authoritarianism," *Vox,* March 1, 2016, accessed June 3, 2016, http://www.vox.com/2016/3/1/11127424/trump-authoritarianism

7. "The Long-Terms Decline in Prime-Age Male Labor Force Participation," *The White House,* June 2016, accessed June 29, 2016, https://www.whitehouse.gov/sites/default/files/page/files/20160620_cea_primeage_male_lfp.pdf

8. Guo, Jeff. "Death Predicts Whether People Vote for Donald Trump," *The Washington Post,* March 4, 2016, accessed May 20, 2016, https://www.washington post.com/news/wonk/wp/2016/03/04/death-predicts-whether-people-vote-for-donald-trump/

9. "'Front Porch Focus Group" Explores Appeal of Trump's Right-Wing Message," *Working America,* January 28, 2016, accessed May 25, 2016, http://www.workingamerica.org/press/releases/Front-Porch-Focus-Group-Explores-Appeal-of-Trump-s-Right-Wing-Message; Frank, Thomas, "Millions of Ordinary Americans Support Donald Trump, Here's Why," *The Guardian,* March 7, 2016, accessed May 25, 2016, https://www.theguardian.com/commentisfree/2016/mar/07/donald-trump-why-americans-support

10. Hetherington, Marc J., and Jonathan D. Weiler. *Authoritarianism and Polarization in American Politics,* New York, NY: Cambridge University Press. 2009.

11. Brownstein, Ronald. "Donald Trump's Coalition of Restoration," *The Atlantic,* June 23, 2016, accessed June 26, 2016, http://www.theatlantic.com/politics/archive/2016/06/donald-trumps-coalition-of-restoration/488345/

12. Donnella, Leah. "Brexit: What's Race Got to Do with It," *NPR,* June 25, 2016, accessed June 26, 2016, http://www.npr.org/sections/codeswitch/2016/06/25/483362200/brexit-whats-race-got-to-do-with-it

13. Taub, Amanda. "The Rise of American Authoritarianism," *Vox,* March 1, 2016, accessed June 27, 2016, http://www.vox.com/2016/3/1/11127424/trump-authoritarianism

14. Ibid.

15. Friedman, Url. "Trust in Government Is Collapsing Around the World," *The Atlantic,* July 5, 2016, accessed July 6, 2016, http://www.govexec.com/management/2016/07/trust-government-collapsing-around-world/129645/?oref=govexec_today_nl

16. "Beyond Distrust: How Americans View Their Government," *Pew Research Centre: U.S. Politics and Policy,* November 23, 2015, accessed June 26, 2016, http://www.people-press.org/2015/11/23/beyond-distrust-how-americans-view-their-government/

17. Ibid.

18. Ibid.

1 Candidate Trump

Resentment in the U.S. and throughout Europe

Globalization has brought complex problems to the U.S. and throughout several democratic countries in Europe that are comparable in many ways. Whereas every country has its own issues, some are strikingly similar: "immigration, integration, jobs, incomes . . . political and business elites."[1] The perceived threat of globalization, feelings of relative economic deprivation, a belief that the political establishment has betrayed the "silent majority," and cultural stress in reaction to an ever-increasing multicultural population have become common grievances. Populism in the U.S. and throughout Europe is rooted in an inability of the general population to accept the ongoing transformation, which is moving the world toward an ever-increasing globalized, multicultural society complete with blurred boundaries and liberal policies. The changes that have occurred, impacting the status quo of the majority of Americans and Europeans, respectively, have occurred at a pace they were not ready for, thus, deepening their cultural stress.

In the last fifty years, both Europe and the U.S. have faced unprecedented transformations. The end of colonialism resulted in the progressive rise of immigration from former colonies in Asia and Africa. Decolonization also caused violent conflicts between and within new nations, resulting in a high volume of refugees fleeing to Europe and America. The fall of the Berlin Wall and the collapse of the Soviet Union further generated a new wave of immigrants, conflicts, and refugees. The creation of the European Union served to blur boundaries between European nations, and its enlargement has led to a complicated process of integration involving the less-developed Eastern European states. The rise of violence in the Middle East, conflicts in North African states—which were left on their own following successive Arab Spring revolutions—and the rise of ISIS have all resulted in an ever-growing number of people fleeing instability, war, and persecution. Moreover, an increase in terrorists acts connected to the growth of Islamic extremism has produced a strong feeling of threat among populations in both the U.S. and Europe.

For many people, these changes have created a deep degree of cultural stress and a feeling that they are losing their privileged or hard-earned social standing. Their anxieties and fears were often incorrectly attributed to bigotry and prejudice and have been continuously ignored by successive leaderships. People feel that political and intellectual elites have defined what is acceptable in terms of their behavior and have prescribed how they should perceive and adhere to particular social challenges. They believe that the purpose of political correctness is to

> tell them what to think, how to regard the political issues of the day, and how they themselves will be regarded if they don't toe the line (racist, homophobe and xenophobe are frequent threatened epithets). . . [is] a blithe disregard for the sensibilities of non-globalist citizens.[2]

In other words, they feel their reactions are not based in bigotry but rather are a response to "the ways outsiders and social changes threaten America."[3]

The critical mass of resentment that has slowly taken shape, as a result, has been further magnified by the slow and uneven recovery from the worldwide economic crisis of 2008 and the resulting high levels of unemployment. One of the perceived answers to this resentment has been to promote the well-being of the nation through a process of closing borders to illegal immigration and supporting exclusive policies of citizenship. This approach is firmly rooted in the nativist belief that cultural heritage, including history, values, and ethnic traditions, is fundamental to any nation and should be protected. It shields a nation from the threats and problems of globalism and mass migration. Voters in the U.S. and across Europe do not believe the current political leadership has been willing or capable of addressing their grievances. "Dissatisfaction, cynicism and outright rejection of traditional political parties"[4] has become more and more dominant across various and diverse populations. Voters are increasingly supportive of nationalist and far right or far left wing populist parties: almost 50 percent in Austria, 29 percent in Switzerland, 21 percent in Denmark, 14 percent in France, and 10 percent in the Netherlands.[5] On June 23, 2016, Great Britain voted to leave the EU, a move that was founded on the belief that doing so would protect the British economy, culture, and way of life from any further threat of immigration. In France, 61 percent of people hold unfavorable views toward the EU, whereas only 38 percent view it favorably. Sixty percent of French people said in 2016 they wished the French government would focus on the country's own problems, as opposed to "helping other countries."[6]

Across the political spectrum throughout Europe, from Italy's leftist Five Star Movement and Slovakia's Direction–Social Democracy to France's right-wing National Front, the Law and Justice Party (PiS) in Poland, and Fidesz in Hungary, populist parties are addressing mounting economic grievances connected with slow economic recovery and global capitalism, as well as increasing fears of immigration.[7] The messages these parties are sending to their respective national electorates rest on several antagonistic dualities. First, they contrast corrupt political elites and the political establishment with the need for people to be represented by authentic leaders. Second, they pit the dominant, culturally homogenous majority, which is typically of native European heritage and mostly raised in the Christian faith, against minorities, such as immigrants and other ethnic, racial, and religious groups, which serves to reinforce xenophobic sentiments. Third, they contrast the interests of the nation and heightened border control with globalization equated with the dissolution of national identity and border permeability. Fourth, they declare "political correctness" and excessive liberal discourse as alien to the general population, which is overregulated and overcontrolled by social taboos.[8] The majority of populist parties, therefore, support the idea of a state founded on a nativist meaning of national identity and, crucially, free of further immigration.

The National Front in France actively promotes anti-elitism and opposes European Union immigration policies, supporting mostly those who are left behind by globalization, including working-class and unemployed populations. Marine Le Pen, the party leader, condemns the French political elite and has described them as pawns of the German government and the European Central Bank. She congratulated her supporters who successfully enabled the party to gain seats in the Senate in the last election: "All of us, together, have blown apart the monopoly of the two parties of the banks, of finance, of multinationals, of giving up, of abandonment . . . But this is only the beginning."[9]

Austria's Freedom Party (FPO) caters to the working class and sends anti-immigrant and anti-Muslim messages, promoting Austrian nationalism. The Polish PiS characterizes Polish national identity as ethnically homogenous and Catholic and aims to protect this vision of national identity from foreign interests. Fidesz in Hungary stresses anti-immigrant and anti-EU rhetoric, while promoting an ethnic concept of Hungarian national identity. Germany's Alternative for Germany (AfD) employs anti-EU sentiments, criticizing the EU bailouts of Greece as well as strong anti-immigrant and anti-Muslim sentiments. AfD has called for preventative measures to be put in place to stop the spread of Islamist ideology in Germany including a ban on the construction of new minarets, emulating a policy adopted in Switzerland years earlier.[10] The Danish People's Party (DPP) opposes multiculturalism and has managed to successfully influence the creation of Denmark's immigration rules and regulations, which are considered to be some of the toughest in Europe. The electoral success of these parties demonstrates how ready populations across Europe are to support a change in liberal immigration and economic policies, as well as limiting the role and power of the EU. The citizens of many of the countries mentioned earlier are further willing to curtail certain freedoms for protection against immigration and Muslims: both PiS and Fidesz have reportedly become increasingly authoritarian, restricting freedom of the press and limiting the rule of law.[11]

America's Election Cycle of 2016

Each election cycle is characterized by some degree of dissatisfaction with the current economic situation facing a country, discontent over social and cultural changes, and frustration with the government policies at the time. Each election cycle, however, has its own specific features defining the election campaigns in significant ways. What are the main characteristics of the current 2016 election cycle?

First, the global economic trend of further outsourcing blue-collar jobs, as well as more knowledge-based jobs, which started in the 1980s and reached its peak in the middle of the 2010s, has had a significant impact. Fifty-three percent of American manufacturing companies and 43 percent of IT companies are currently outsourcing their jobs to foreign countries.[12] There has been a steady decline of nearly 5.5 million manufacturing jobs over the last twenty-five years. Around twenty million people have to change their jobs annually due to layoffs and plant closures.[13] Moreover, to China alone, the U.S. has lost 3.2 million jobs over the last fifteen years.[14] Many of these jobs were in factories that manufactured toys, clothing, and furniture and in other labor-intensive relatively low-skilled industries. The impact of these processes has been felt most severely by White, working-class men: their involvement in the workforce has decreased from 88 percent in 1954 to 72 percent in 2016. Job opportunities in manufacturing industries have dropped significantly in the last fifteen years: in Pennsylvania, for example, manufacturing employment decreased from nine hundred thousand in 2000 to less than six hundred thousand in 2015.[15]

Rural areas that are homes to small industries have been hit the hardest by deindustrialization.[16] Industrial jobs are more important for rural America because post-industrial options for rural people are far fewer than for metropolitan Americans.[17] People in rural areas feel more resentment toward people who live in cities because of the opportunities provided to these urban settings and because they believe that they have less power, less public funds, and are not respected in the same way as people living in urban settings.[18]

The highest unemployment rate is found in small, former industrial centers where a decline in industries such as mining and long-struggling agricultural economies has been most acute.[19] Overall, only 27 percent of Americans believe the country is going in the right direction, whereas 67 percent think it is on the wrong track.[20]

Second, the income gap between rich and poor is currently at its widest in recent U.S. history. Since the 1970s, less progressive taxes and stagnant wage growth has led to increased income and wealth inequality: the wealthiest 160,000 families own as much wealth as the poorest 145 million families, and that wealth is about ten times as unequal as income.[21] Since the Great Recession of 2009, the U.S. economy has been growing, but the incomes of different social classes have not grown comparably. Between 2009 and 2012, the top one percent of the American population captured 95 percent of the total income growth.[22] In comparison, the typical American family now receives less income—adjusted for inflation—than the typical family did fifteen years ago, a trend that hasn't been seen since the Great Depression.[23] Government support for low-income families has declined from 50 percent of transfer payments in 1979 to about 35 percent in 2007. This change reflects an increase in spending for programs focused on the growing elderly population in America (such as Social Security and Medicare).[24] In addition, the younger generation—typically better educated than their parents—is falling farther behind their parents' generation in most measures of economic well-being.[25] Moreover, because of their involvement in half-time jobs, the median income of households in the bottom third of the population in 2014 was $24,000, just a little more than a quarter of the median of $90,000 for the top two-thirds.[26] Poor and near-poor Whites are the most unhappy and desperate group in the U.S.[27] Over the last fifteen years, there has been a significant increase in deaths from suicide and substance abuse for American Whites aged from forty-five to fifty-four years old.[28]

The American Dream of social mobility has increasingly become an illusion. The most important predictors of success in the U.S. are the wealth and privileges conferred by parents and ancestors. Class-zoned neighborhoods, private education, better access to economic tools, such as loans and trusts, create clear distinctions and, ultimately, more barriers to upward mobility. The stigma of the "White trash" label, along with references to lower levels of education, White anger, and ignorance created a biased perception of blue-collar workers as an "embarrassing social phenomena."[29] The elites have blamed them for the inability to be successful and promote a better future for their children. Approximately three-quarters of Americans held the firm belief that the American Dream meant "being free to accomplish anything through hard work," and about 90 percent said hard work and having ambition were either essential or very important to getting ahead in life.[30] Thus White blue-collar workers' poverty has been attributed to their own failure rather than to class barriers having made the dream of upward mobility unobtainable.

Third, the changing racial composition of the country—the new generation of millennials is 55.8 percent White and 44.2 percent non-White, with nearly 30 percent "new minorities" (Hispanics, Asians, and those identifying as two or more races)[31]—has contributed to a growing feeling of cultural and racial stress among White Americans who have lower access to jobs and to elite education.

> The angriest and most pessimistic people in America are the people we used to call Middle Americans. Middle-class and middle-aged; not rich and not poor; people who are irked when asked to press 1 for English, and who wonder how *white male* became an accusation rather than a description.[32]

They connect the decline in employment opportunities and American culture with expanded immigration. Only 33 percent of Americans are satisfied with the current immigration situation.[33] Sixty-six percent of those who identify with Republicans state that immigrants create serious problems for the U.S.[34] They also think the American way of life and culture generally has gotten worse since the 1950s because of immigrants. They strongly dislike immigrants who do not speak English but receive equal educational, economic, and social benefits. In 2016, 50 percent of Americans surveyed thought race relations in America were getting worse in comparison to 30 percent in 2014.[35] Almost half of the U.S. population thinks President Obama has driven those of different races farther apart.[36] Many White Americans believe they are experiencing increased reverse discrimination. The increasing diversity of the U.S. has created the opposing phenomenon: "many White Americans are confronting race in a way they have never had to before."[37] This change in racial status has led to frustration and a fear among White, working-class Americans of becoming a social minority.[38]

Fourth, Islamic extremism is seen as a major threat to the U.S. Eighty percent of the American public believe ISIS is a major threat to the well-being of the U.S., and 55 percent see refugees leaving countries such as Iraq and Syria as a major threat. Among Republicans, these numbers are much higher: 93 percent of them consider ISIS and 80 percent consider refugees as major threats.[39] People are afraid of possible terrorism, and their fears are reinforced by the 2015–2016 terrorist acts in the U.S., Europe, and North Africa. In the light of these attacks, people have become more supportive of more restrictive and aggressive immigration policies. More specifically, people become more susceptible to the need for "authoritarian thinking" when they feel their safety is under threat.[40]

Fifth, political polarization in the U.S. is at its highest in recent history. The average partisan gap has nearly doubled over the last twenty-five years—from ten percentage points in 1987 to eighteen percentage points today. Whereas membership in both parties has decreased, both parties have become more uniformed in their ideology. The percentage of Democrats who are liberal on all or most value dimensions has nearly doubled from just 30 percent in 1994 to 56 percent today; the percentage of conservatives in the Republican Party increased from 45 percent in 1994 to 53 percent today.[41] "Republicans are most distinguished by their increasingly minimalist views about the role of government and lack of support for environmentalism. Democrats have become more socially liberal and secular."[42] Assessments of the opposing political party have also become more negative.[43] Currently, 43 percent of Republicans have a highly negative opinion of the Democratic Party and 38 percent of Democrats feel very unfavorably toward the GOP.[44] Some scholars suggest that this political polarization is connected to another trend discussed earlier: the widening gap between the rich and the poor.[45]

Political polarization affects people's assessment of presidential candidates. Many voters make a choice not based on their like of a candidate but rather their strong dislike of another. Among Clinton supporters, the Democratic front-runner, 58 percent support her because they strongly like Clinton and 30 percent because they strongly dislike Trump.[46] Forty-seven percent of Trump supporters are motivated by the slogan "Never Hillary." Scott Reed, a political strategist for the U.S. Chamber of Commerce noted, whereas there remain "many unknowns" about Trump, "the knowns about Hillary are very powerful motivators to Republicans."[47] Senator Rubio, who strongly criticized Trump as a "fraud" and a "con artist"[48] during his own run for presidency confirmed his willingness to support Trump as nominee in order to stop Clinton.

Sixth, voters in the U.S. exhibit a particularly low degree of trust in their politicians and their ability or willingness to change the situation facing the U.S., in addition to addressing the major issues concerning the public. Eighty percent of voters agree with the statement, "It's time to try something new" by electing a president who is "committed to common sense, values, civility, and working to get things done."[49] Americans, therefore, are looking for a candidate outside the usual pool of career politicians. As Sarah Palin, a 2008 vice presidential candidate, said in her speech endorsing Trump, "We need someone new, who has the power, and is in the position to bust up the establishment to make things great again."[50]

The Republican Party, as a whole, has seemed unprepared to respond to these grievances. The idea of Reaganism with its anti-Soviet internationalism, social conservatism, and economic agenda of tax cuts, budget cuts, deregulation, free trade, and welcoming immigration policy dominated the

Republican Party until the start of the race for the presidency in 2015. For several decades, the working class aligned with the GOP mainly because of economic and cultural concerns. Economic stresses associated with the Great Recession of 2008—economic frustration and unwillingness to accept cuts in social security programs—however, have triggered the White working class to move away from Republican elites.[51] The GOP elite has failed to address these major grievances in American society: inequality and continued wage stagnation, the need for the protection of social benefits, and health care for the middle class who did not want it to be taken from them and redistributed "to Americans who are newer, poorer, and in their view less deserving, in Barack Obama's words, to 'spread the wealth around.'"[52]

Presidential candidate Donald Trump does not seem to be genuinely invested in Reagan's legacy. He does not demonstrate consistent support for conservative values. Only 13 percent of his total supporters consider themselves very conservative.[53] Nor are they highly religious or strictly attached to conservative policies or the memory of Ronald Reagan.[54] Trump's independence from Republican donors has given him an opportunity to move away from the three pillars of traditional Republicanism: libertarian economics, social conservatism, and militarism.[55] Instead, he has sought to address the major grievances of the working class: their economic insecurity and their growing economic nationalism. He has promised to protect them from establishment policies—outsourcing American jobs and open immigration policies that impact their wages—as well as Democratic policies of welcoming refugees and promoting minorities.

How Different are the Two Candidates in Addressing These Issues?

Donald Trump and Hillary Clinton differ both in style and their positions on major issues. First, Trump rarely goes into detail; rather, he states his positions sharply, making quick diagnoses and bold promises. Clinton, on the other hand, often provides comprehensive strategies and complex solutions but does not have a strong emotional appeal among the wider public. She presents herself as an empathic listener who pays attention to peoples' needs and who seeks to tailor her speeches to the needs of a particular audience. "Speaking on policy, Trump is a dry-erase board, while Clinton is a Talmud portion; his most specific ideas are haphazard doodles while her remarks are often larded with so much marginalia that her footnotes have footnotes."[56]

Second, Trump has advocated for a total overhaul of domestic and international policies. He has described the current situation America finds herself in as economically disastrous and that the solution demands a completely new political approach. Trump has promised to lead the nation and "Make

America great again" because "We never win, anymore" and "America is in bad shape." From the beginning, Trump has put himself at the center of his campaign strategy and has sought to craft the impression that solving the nation's problems will be an easy job for him. Conversely, Clinton, as a professional politician, has promoted the need to change the system from within. She has advocated for incremental change rather than dramatic transformation.

Third, Trump's political approach has placed nationalism at the heart of his campaign. He does not believe America benefits from international trade agreements and the promise of the global economy. In his foreign policy speech on April 27, 2016, Trump stated, "We will no longer surrender this country or its people to the false song of globalism . . . I am skeptical of international unions that tie us up and bring America down."[57] He believes that the nation "remains the true foundation of happiness and harmony."[58] Clinton, however, advocates for globalism: supporting the rights and well-being of people all over the world, the dissolution of social boundaries, and the global economy. For Clinton, it is in the American national interest to be involved in global politics and global partnerships. She views the U.S. as a world player with the ability to set the agenda for the international community. "Hillary Clinton . . . is the personification of the globalist elite—generally open borders, humanitarian interventionist, traditionally a free trader."[59]

Fourth, for both candidates, their individual areas of strengths are the areas of weaknesses of the other. Trump is rated highly among his supporters on the issue of authenticity. His voters believe in his genuineness, independence, and ability to "tells it as it is." These are not traits highly associated with Clinton; instead, many voters have expressed severe doubt concerning her honesty and independence. Voters who value experience in their candidates are, however, supportive of Clinton and have reservations about Trump's ability to rise to be president.

Fifth, Trump is much more conservative on issues pertaining to the rights of individuals and the role of the state than Clinton with most disagreements occurring over the issues of abortion, same-sex marriage, and environmental protection regulations. Trump is supportive of the fossil fuel industry and has expressed skepticism about the economic viability of renewable energy, which is keenly promoted by Clinton.[60] They also completely disagree on the effectiveness of stricter punishment for criminals, legal status pathways for illegal immigrants, prioritizing Social Security, and gun ownership rights.[61]

Trump, for example, has created the impression among his supporters that fixing the American health-care system would be an easy task. Clinton, with her experience of helping to craft a new health insurance program, has stressed the enormity of the task at hand. Trump strongly opposes gun control and has been endorsed by the NRA. Clinton, however, supports universal background checks on all gun purchases and an increased responsibility to be placed on the manufacturers of guns and those who sell them.

Both candidates have promised to reverse the decades of free trade that has led to millions of American jobs being shipped overseas because of the advantages of cheap, foreign labor, but their approaches differ. Trump has emphasized lowering taxes:

> Under the Trump plan, America will compete with the world and win by cutting the corporate tax rate to 15%, taking our rate from one of the worst to one of the best . . . A one-time deemed repatriation of corporate cash held overseas at a significantly discounted 10% tax rate.[62]

On his campaign website, Trump lists four ways he would reform trade with China to keep jobs and factories in the U.S. These include declaring China as a currency manipulator, ending its intellectual property violations, eliminating its illegal export subsidies, and lowering the U.S. corporate tax rate to 15 percent to stop businesses from moving abroad. He also floated a plan to impose a 45 percent tariff on Chinese exports to the U.S. in a meeting with the *New York Times* editorial board. Clinton, however, has stressed the need to improve the skills of American workers as a resolution to this problem.

> Americans need to be able to get ahead and stay ahead—that means putting the next generation of well-paying jobs within reach for everyone who is willing to work hard. Hillary believes that every American—especially young people—should be able to learn the skills they need to get hired, seize new opportunities at work, get promoted, and contribute in a 21st-century workforce.[63]

Trump's proposals are easier for voters to comprehend, and, most importantly, they do not require additional education, as Clinton has recommended. Simply put, the American electorate need merely elect a leader who will punish everyone who has been taking jobs away from the American working class.

Is Trump Manipulative or Genuine?

To better comprehend the Trump effect, it is important to understand if Trump's actions are "natural," based on his instinctive reaction to the issues facing American society, or "professional," based on his business skills and knowledge that allow him to instrumentally manipulate the desires of large segments of the American populace and respond to the needs of his followers. It is not the author's intention to speculate on this issue. Unlike many recent publications, the premise of this book is not to put Trump "on a couch" or provide a psychoanalytical review of his writings and speeches. Instead, to answer this particular question, my methodology is to analyze the opinions of people who are close to him as well as his own statements about successful political campaigns. This approach will provide the reader with insights into Trump as a candidate, shedding some light on the question of whether his campaign is thoughtfully crafted or based on off-the-cuff intuition.

Some insights can be found in interviews with former contestants of *The Apprentice.* Many of them believe Trump, as a savvy businessman and smart marketer, knows how to address the grievances and needs of America and her citizens in the most effective way. As one former contestant stated, "I will say he is smart and I do believe that he does know what he's saying and I do believe he does know why he's saying it. He knows exactly the audience he's going after."[64] Another contestant echoed this sentiment, stating,

> There's a fundamental misunderstanding of just the amount of xenophobia within the Republican party. And I think that Donald Trump has picked up on it and he's tapped it. That's what he does. What a brilliant marketer does is they tap into people's concerns, desires, and they speak to them. Fear sells. Fear has always sold, but so does optimism. So he's literally selling both.[65]

Former contestants also highlighted Trump's personal style of being tough and forthright, which have been continually reflected in the tactics he has been employing during the race for the presidency. As one contestant noted,

> Donald Trump knows what he wants, and he knows how to get it. He does not beat around the bush, and he takes no prisoners. Be that as that may, that is who he is and that's how he became so successful, and that's why I think he's doing well in the political realm—he's a breath of fresh air in a sort of stale and broken system.[66]

Another contestant validated this position, stating,

> He's not gonna bullshit you. He's gonna say what's on his mind. Does he get a little bit harsh sometimes? He does. Yes, he can be a little bit brash, but it's refreshing! I know he's going get the job done, he's not going to bullshit you. People are so brainwashed into thinking that he's gonna blow up our country because he's gonna piss somebody off. It's not going to happen.[67]

In his 2000 book *The America We Deserve*, Trump clearly describes what type of candidate is needed to win over the majority of voters.

> I am definitely a different look. I'm not prepackaged. I'm not plastic. I'm not script. And I am not 'handled.' I tell you what I think. It's quite a departure from the usual office-seeking pols. Maybe the voters will find it refreshing. I guarantee you one thing, they'd find it interesting. After two years of George W. Bush, John McCain, Al Gore, and Bill Bradley running for president, the voters will be bored to death. They'll be looking for a candidate who is straight talking, straight shooting, beholden to no one, and has proven that he actually get things done.

In this passage, Trump outlines the guidelines for a successful campaign: (1) offer oneself as an alternative to establishment career politicians, (2) emphasize authenticity and independence, (3) go beyond typical electoral rhetoric and political correctness (as he notes in his book, "people want fresh answers"), (4) be straightforward and clear on the issues important to voters, (5) emphasize your ability to get things done, and, finally, (6) be entertaining and funny.

During the speech in which he announced his bid for presidency on June 16, 2015, Trump addressed all of his original recommendations.[68] First, he underlined how different he was in comparison to the established political leadership and the career politicians who were his presidential competitors. He stressed they had continually misled people and hadn't produced any real solutions to the huge problems facing America: "Politicians are all talk, no action. Nothing's gonna get done. They will not bring us—believe me—to the promised land. They will not." He continued, stressing that the American population was completely dissatisfied with political demagogy:

> I watch the speeches of these people, and they say the sun will rise, the moon will set, all sorts of wonderful things will happen. And people are saying, "What's going on? I just want a job. Just get me a job. I don't need the rhetoric. I want a job."

Second, Trump emphasized his independence, noting he neither answers to lobbyists nor promotes the interests of big donors. Speaking plainly about politicians, Trump stated, "They're controlled fully—they're controlled fully by the lobbyists, by the donors, and by the special interests, fully . . . We have to stop, and it has to stop now." Addressing free trade, Trump said, "We have people that are controlled by special interests. And it's just not going to work." Comparing himself to these politicians, Trump emphasized his independence: "I'm using my own money. I'm not using the lobbyists. I'm not using donors. I don't care. I'm really rich."

Third, in order to provide "fresh" answers to the range of issues facing Americans and their country today, Trump has sought to go beyond the typical responses to these problems by casting off the shackles of political correctness. For example, Trump has denied government statistics concerning the American unemployment rate: "And our real unemployment is anywhere from 18 to 20 percent. Don't believe the 5.6. Don't believe it." On the issue of immigration, Trump referred to illegal Mexican immigrants as rapists and criminals, highlighting a recent report that 80 percent of Central American women and girls are raped crossing into the U.S.[69] Lastly, Trump attacked the current secretary of state, John Kerry, stating, "Secretary Kerry . . . has absolutely no concept of negotiation, [he's] making a horrible and laughable deal" with Iran.

Fourth, Trump has demonstrated his love for plainly spoken rhetoric and simple solutions to entrenched issues. At the beginning of his candidacy announcement speech, Trump opted for a straightforward statement that America was not a great country anymore: "Our country is in serious trouble. We don't have victories anymore. We used to have victories, but we don't have them." Trump accentuated many domestic and international threats he attributed to the diminishing strength of the U.S. He presented Mexico as an enemy: "When do we beat Mexico at the border? They're laughing at us, at our stupidity. And now they are beating us economically. They are not our friend, believe me." He completely disavowed the Affordable Care Act: "We have a disaster called the big lie: Obamacare . . . You have to be hit by a tractor, literally, a tractor, to use it, because the deductibles are so high, it's virtually useless." Finally, he stated that he would exercise this straightforward approach: "This is going to be an election that's based on competence, because people are tired of these nice people."

Fifth, Trump has continually emphasized his ability to successfully and decisively address every problem facing America. He stated, "We need a leader that wrote *The Art of the Deal*. We need a leader that can bring back our jobs, can bring back our manufacturing, can bring back our military, can take care of our vets." He continued,

> We need somebody that can take the brand of the United States and make it great again. It's not great again. We need—we need somebody—we need somebody that literally will take this country and make it great again. We can do that.

He has also provided examples pertaining to specific issues. "When was the last time anybody saw us beating, let's say, China in a trade deal? They kill us. I beat China all the time. All the time." Similarly, Trump has stated that he would be able to resolve the complicated issue of health care:

> We have to repeal Obamacare, and it can be—and—and it can be replaced with something much better for everybody. Let it be for everybody. But

much better and much less expensive for people and for the government. And we can do it.

Additionally, Trump has promised to resolve international trade issues: "I know the negotiators in the world, and I put them one for each country. Believe me, folks. We will do very, very well, very, very well" and "I will stop Iran from getting nuclear weapons."

Sixth, he has entertained the public by insulting political leaders and the heads of international corporations.

> You looked at (Jeb) Bush, it took him five days to answer the question on Iraq. He couldn't answer the question. He didn't know. I said, "Is he intelligent?" Then I looked at Rubio. He was unable to answer the question, is Iraq a good thing or bad thing? He didn't know. He couldn't answer the question.

Describing a hypothetical discussion on outsourcing jobs to Mexico with the leadership of Ford Motor Company, Trump amused the audience by noting,

> The head of Ford will call me back, I would say, within an hour after I told them the bad news. But it could be he'd want to be cool, and he'll wait until the next day. You know, they want to be a little cool. And he'll say, "Please, please, please." He'll beg for a little while, and I'll say, "No interest."

Another piece of advice Trump-the-presidential-hopeful is taking from Trump-the-businessman is how to deal with the media. In *The Art of the Deal*, Trump writes,

> One thing I've learned about the press is that they're always hungry for a good story, and the more sensational the better. It's in the nature of the job, and I understand that. The point is that if you are a little different, or a little outrageous, or if you do things that are bold or controversial, the press is going to write about you. I've always done things a little differently, I don't mind controversy, and my deals tend to be somewhat ambitious. Also, I achieved a lot when I was very young, and I chose to live in a certain style. The result is that the press has always wanted to write about me.[70]

Trump's statements on a majority of social issues have been "bold or controversial." Many journalists consider them "outrageous" or at least "different." As a result, Trump has received nearly $2 billion in free media coverage, more than any of the other candidates on either side of the political aisle.[71] News and commentary about his campaign on television, in newspapers and magazines, and on social media have appeared twice as often as that of former secretary of state Hillary Clinton, the Democratic front-runner, and six times more often than that of Republican candidate Senator Ted Cruz.[72] These statistics have been garnered from the new real-time tools for observing media ratings. These modern analytical tools show publications about Trump attract more attention than those about his opponents. A comparative analysis shows the media representing Trump more frequently than other candidates. The chairman of CBS, Leslie Moonves, said that Trump's candidacy: "may not be good for America, but it's damn good for CBS." Ross Douthat of the *New York Times* likewise remarked, Trump is "such a gift to our industry." Moreover, Trump actively uses new media—he has 9.3 million Twitter followers and has received 9.4 million Facebook likes. This strategy has contributed to the popularity of his image among supporters.

A comparison of Trump's statements and his actions on the campaign trail has shown his political positions are instrumental, which have helped him to gain more popular support. For example, Trump has stated he is "not a believer"[73] in global warming and has referred to the issue as "a total hoax,"[74] "bullshit"[75] created by the Chinese to "make U.S. manufacturing non-competitive."[76] Recently, however, he has applied for "permission to erect a coastal protection works to prevent erosion at his seaside golf resort, Trump International Golf Links and Hotel Ireland in County Clare."[77]

This book is, therefore, based on the assumption that Trump's campaign has been crafted out of his marketing and business skills. During his campaign, Trump has recognized where and with whom he can get the most return on his investment: his tweets and comments during the campaign. He clearly understands there is a general malaise in the U.S. and has sought to create a space for people to express certain views and frustrations more openly. Due to the predominant influence and perceived rise of political correctness in American society, such views have not been expressed as openly in previous election cycles.

Notes

1. Henley, Jon, Helena Bengtsson, and Caelainn Barr. "Across Europe, Distrust of Mainstream Political Parties Is on the Rise," *The Guardian*, May 25, 2016, accessed May 25, 2016, https://www.theguardian.com/world/2016/may/25/across-europe-distrust-of-mainstream-political-parties-is-on-the-rise
2. Merry, Robert W. "Trump vs. Hillary Is Nationalism vs. Globalism, 2016," *The National Interest*, May 4, 2016, accessed May 18, 2016, http://nationalinterest.org.mutex.gmu.edu/feature/trump-vs-hillary-nationalism-vs-globalism-2016–16041?page=2

3. Taub, Amanda. "The Rise of American Authoritarianism."
4. Adler, Katya. "Is Europe Lurching to the Far Right?" *BBC*, April 28, 2016, accessed (May 25, 2016), http://www.bbc.com/news/world-europe-36150807
5. Ibid.
6. le Corre, Philippe. "The Brexit Contagion could Consume the French Elite Next," *Brookings*, June 30, 2016, accessed (May 23, 2016), http://www.brookings.edu/blogs/order-from-chaos/posts/2016/06/30-brexit-is-france-next-lecorre?utm_campaign=Brookings+Brief&utm_source=hs_email&utm_medium=email&utm_content=31214262&_hsenc=p2ANqtz—1v4iLRvz4eryd3Pafb1QDfJBDT3ZcdVyvaltvd3IrZEfN3tb12f_7ucbt45NUypQlv_NmUbLYP5CwdTXlqzx5wVczoQ&_hsmi=31214262
7. Frum, David. "The Great Republican Revolt," *The Atlantic*, January/February 2016 issue, accessed April 29, 2016, http://www.theatlantic.com/magazine/archive/2016/01/the-great-republican-revolt/419118/
8. Wodak, Ruth, Majid KhosraviNik, and Brigitte Mral. *Right-Wing Populism in Europe: Politics and Discourse*. A&C Black, 2013.
9. Farago, James. "Comparative Far Right Politics, US and Europe," *The Guardian*, April 26, 2012, accessed May 28, 2016, https://www.theguardian.com/commentisfree/cifamerica/2012/apr/26/comparative-far-right-politics-us-europe
10. Greven, Thomas. "The Rise of Right-Wing Populism in Europe and the United States: A Comparative Perspective," *Friedrich, Ebert, Stiftung*, May 2016, accessed June 2, 2016, http://www.fesdc.org/fileadmin/user_upload/publications/Rightwing Populism.pdf
11. Ibid.
12. Statistic Brain Staff. "Job Overseas Outsourcing Statistics," *Statistic Brain*, accessed June 28, 2016, http://www.statisticbrain.com/outsourcing-statistics-by-country/
13. Luhby, Tami. "Why It Would be Tough for Trump to Bring Jobs Back from China," *CNN Money*, February 12, 2016, accessed June 5, 2016, http://money.cnn.com/2016/02/12/news/economy/donald-trump-china-mexico-jobs/
14. Manning, Stephan, and Marcus Larsen. "Trump and Clinton Want to Bring Back Millions of Outsourced Jobs," *Government Executive*, May 29, 2016, accessed May 30, 2016, http://www.govexec.com/management/2016/05/trump-and-clinton-wantto-bring-back-millions-outsourced-jobs-heres-why-they-cant/128531/?oref=site-govexec-flyin-sailthru
15. Chen, Victor T. "Manufacturing Employment (United States)," *Victor Tan Chen*, April 25, 2016, accessed June 6, 2016, https://victortanchen.com/manufacturing-employment-united-states/
16. Cole, Peter. "A Tale of Two Towns: Globalization and Rural Deindustrialization in the US." *WorkingUSA* 12, no. 4, 2009.
17. Thomas J. Sugrue, *The Origins of the Urban Crisis: Race and Inequality in Postwar Detroit*. Princeton: Princeton University Press, 1996.
18. Cramer, Kathrine. "The Politics of Resentment: Trump Says What Angry Voters Think," *The Chronicle of Higher Education*, June 19, 2016, accessed June 26, 2016, http://chronicle.com.mutex.gmu.edu/article/The-Politics-of-Resentment/236818?cid=cp43
19. Berube, Alan. "Where Are the Nonworking Prime-Age Men?" *Brookings*, June 21, 2016. accessed June 25, 2016, http://www.brookings.edu/blogs/the-avenue/posts/2016/06/21-nonworking-prime-age-men-berube?utm_campaign=Brookings+Brief&utm_source=hs_email&utm_medium=email&utm_content=30912090&_

hsenc=p2ANqtz-_AGwbffkISMay_7Vq9h1–0QEDelzjCihGzoaJ5po41EnUzDO
Ayb5d2wiGvzWGNK4pbMaEFC1d0QCa-Y6DlY_0bNqeLYw&_hsmi=30912090
20. Huffpost Pollster Staff. "Poll Chart: US Right Direction Wrong Track," *Huffpost Pollster*, updated continually, accessed June 28, 2016, http://elections.huffington post.com/pollster/us-right-direction-wrong-track?version=meter+at+6&module =meter-Links&pgtype=article&contentId=&mediaId=&referrer=&priority=true &action=click&contentCollection=meter-links-click
21. Matthews, Chris. "Wealth Inequality in America: It's Worse than You Think," *Fortune*, October 31, 2014, accessed June 3, 2016, http://fortune.com/2014/10/31/ inequality-wealth-income-us/
22. Sommeiller, Estelle, and Mark Price. "The Increasingly Unequal States of America," *Economic Policy Institute*, January 26, 2015, accessed June 19, 2016, http:// www.epi.org/publication/income-inequality-by-state-1917-to-2012/
23. Leonhardt, David. "The Great Wage Slowdown of the 21st Century," *New York Times*, October 7, 2014, accessed June 9, 2016, http://www.nytimes. com/2014/10/07/upshot/the-great-wage-slowdown-of-the-21st-century. html?smid=tw-share&abt=0002&abg=0&version=meter+at+8&module=meter-Links&pgtype=article&contentId=&mediaId=&referrer=&priority=true&actio n=click&contentCollection=meter-links-click
24. Matthews, Chris. "4 Things You Didn't (but Should) Know About Economic Inequality," *Fortune*, June 11, 2015, accessed June 19, 2016, http://fortune. com/2015/06/11/income-inequality/
25. Ibid.
26. Sawhill, Isabel V., Nathan Joo, and Edward Rodrigue. "To Help Low-Income American Households, We Have to Close the 'Work Gap,'" *Brookings*, May 31, 2016, accessed June 18, 2016, http://www.brookings.edu/blogs/ social-mobility-memos/posts/2016/05/31-help-low-income-close-work-gap-sawhill?utm_campaign=Brookings+Brief&utm_source=hs_email&utm_ medium=email&utm_content=30131225&_hsenc=p2ANqtz-8yKJcZrgHBS F0RV14xDnsh12mCUV28IN_KEQ34Ep4Uk49yq8ucNbbDOwiQGG0HW7p k0owQBJbComJYRsbnSUdI9qwuOg&_hsmi=30131225
27. Packer, George. *The Unwinding: An Inner History of the New America*. Macmillan, 2013.
28. Case, Anne, and Angus Deaton. "Rising morbidity and mortality in midlife among white non-Hispanic Americans in the 21st century." *Proceedings of the National Academy of Sciences* 112, no. 49 (2015): 15078–15083.
29. Isenberg, Nancy. *White Trash: The 400-Year Untold History of Class in America*. Penguin, 2016.
30. Economic Mobility Project. "Opinion Poll on Economic Mobility and the American Dream," *The Pew Charitable Trusts*, March 12, 2009, accessed June 22, 2016, http://www.pewtrusts.org/en/research-and-analysis/analysis/2009/03/12/ opinion-poll-on-economic-mobility-and-the-american-dream
31. Frey, William H. "Diversity Defines the Millennial Generation," *Brookings*, June 28, 2016, accessed June 28, 2016, http://www.brookings.edu/blogs/the-avenue/ posts/2016/06/28-diversity-millennial-frey?utm_campaign=Brookings+Brief& utm_source=hs_email&utm_medium=email&utm_content=31112059&_ hsenc=p2ANqtz-8kjavWGHB1—gzoDgpGpim8lnp_bmfxdeHo6xMfdEbhpS fX9Oa1mamkMM1id1SVV7wUxHRBvDK9T0H-LIZS169z6pkKA&_ hsmi=31112059

32. Frum, David. "The Great Republican Revolt," *The Atlantic*, January/February 2016 issue. accessed June 29, 2016, http://www.theatlantic.com/magazine/archive/2016/01/the-great-republican-revolt/419118/
33. Newport, Frank. "American Public Opinion and Immigration," *Gallup*, July 20, 2015, accessed June 27, 2016, http://www.gallup.com/opinion/polling-matters/184262/american-public-opinion-immigration.aspx
34. Cooper, Betsy, Daniel Cox, Rachel Lienesch, and Robert P. Jones. "Anxiety, Nostalgia, and Mistrust: Finds from the 2015 American Values Survey," *PRRI*, November 17, 2015, accessed June 27, 2016, http://publicreligion.org/research/2015/11/survey-anxiety-nostalgia-and-mistrust-findings-from-the-2015-american-values-survey/#.Vzn6numKn8E
35. Rasmussen Reports Staff. "50% Say Race Relations in America Getting Worse," *Rasmussen Reports*, January 19, 2016, accessed June 26, 2016, http://www.rasmussenreports.com/public_content/lifestyle/general_lifestyle/january_2016/50_say_race_relations_in_america_getting_worse
36. Rasmussen Reports Staff. "Has Obama Widened the Racial Divide?" *Rasmussen Reports*, September 4, 2015, accessed June 26, 2016, http://www.rasmussenreports.com/public_content/politics/general_politics/august_2015/has_obama_widened_the_racial_divide
37. Taub, Amanda. "The Rise of American Authoritarianism."
38. Craig, Maureen A., and Jennifer A. Richeson. "On the Precipice of a 'Majority-Minority' America: Perceived Status Threat from the Racial Demographic Shift Affects White Americans' Political Ideology." *Psychological Science*, 2014 vol. 25 no. 6 1189–1197.
39. Pew Research Center Staff. "Public Uncertain, Divided Over America's Place in the World." *Pew research Center: U.S. Politics & Policy*, May 5, 2016. accessed May 7, 2016, http://www.people-press.org/2016/05/05/3-international-threats-defense-spending/
40. Hetherington, M., and Suhay, E. "Authoritarianism, Threat, and Americans' Support for the War on Terror." *American Journal of Political Science*, 55, (2011): 546–560.
41. Doherty, Carroll. "Which Party Is More to Blame for Political Polarization? It Depends on the Measure," *Pew research Center*, June 17, 2016, accessed June 17, 2016, http://www.pewresearch.org/fact-tank/2014/06/17/which-party-is-more-to-blame-for-political-polarization-it-depends-on-the-measure/
42. Pew Research Centre Staff. "Trends in American Values: 1987–2012," *The Pew research Center: For The People & the Press*, June 4, 2012, accessed June 28, 2016, http://www.people-press.org/files/legacy-pdf/06–04–12%20Values%20Release.pdf?version=meter+at+6&module=meter-Links&pgtype=article&contentId=&mediaId=&referrer=&priority=true&action=click&content Collection=meter-links-click
43. Iyengar, Shanto, Gaurav Sood, and Yphtach Lelkes. "Affect, not ideology a social identity perspective on polarization." *Public Opinion Quarterly* 76, no. 3 (2012): 405–431.
44. Doherty. "Which Party Is More to Blame for Political Polarization?"
45. Swanson, Ana. "These Political Scientists May Have Just Discovered Why U.S. Politics Are a Disaster," *The Washington Post*, October 7, 2015, accessed June 25, 2016, https://www.washingtonpost.com/news/wonk/wp/2015/10/07/these-political-scientists-may-have-discovered-the-real-reason-u-s-politics-are-a-disaster/

46. Bump, Philip. "How Likely Are Bernie Sanders Supporters to Actually Vote for Donald Trump? Here are some clues," *The Washington Post*, May 24, 2016, accessed June 2, 2016, https://www.washingtonpost.com/news/the-fix/wp/2016/05/24/how-likely-are-bernie-sanders-supporters-to-actually-vote-for-donald-trump-here-are-some-clues

47. Bykowicz, Julie, and Julie Pace. "Never Mind Trump, GOP Uniting under Banner: 'Never Hillary,'" *Associated Press*, May 27, 2016, accessed May 28, 2016, http://bigstory.ap.org/article/2490bac92e6f43ff931e45d40cf21bd3/never-hillary-unites-republicans-squeamish-about-trump

48. Spiering, Charlie. "Marco Rubio Strikes Again: Donald Trump A 'Fraud' and A 'Con Artist,'" *Breitbart*, February 26, 2016, accessed April 6, 2016, http://www.breitbart.com/big-government/2016/02/26/marco-rubio-strikes-again-donald-trump-a-fraud-and-a-con-artist/

49. Schoen, Douglas E. "Clinton vs. Trump Makes Many Americans Unhappy. Here's What Voters Really Want in 2016," *Fox News: Opinion*, May 26, 2016, accessed May 26, 2016, http://www.foxnews.com/opinion/2016/05/26/clinton-vs-trump-makes-many-americans-unhappy-heres-what-voters-really-want-in-2016.html

50. Deckman, Melissa. "Some Women Actually Do Support Donald Trump. Here's Why," *The Washington Post*, April 7, 2016, accessed May 28, 2016, https://www.washingtonpost.com/news/monkey-cage/wp/2016/04/07/some-women-actually-do-support-donald-trump-heres-why/

51. Galston, William A. "How Trump Killed Reaganism," *The Wall Street Journal*, April 27, 2016, accessed June 7, 2016, http://www.wsj.com/articles/how-trump-killed-reaganism-1461711203

52. Obamamania. "Obama—Spread the Wealth Around," YouTube, October 13, 2008, accessed May 19, 2016, https://www.youtube.com/watch?v=OoqI5PSRcXM

53. Brady, David W., and Douglas Rivers. "Who Are Trump's Supporters?" *Real-Clear Politics*, September 9, 2015, accessed June 28, 2016, http://www.realclearpolitics.com/articles/2015/09/09/who_are_trumps_supporters.html

54. Lowry, Richard. "How Trump Killed the Reagan Mystique," *Politico*, March 2, 2016, accessed June 9, 2016, http://www.politico.com/magazine/story/2016/03/how-trump-killed-the-reagan-mystique-213696#ixzz4AMZSKKVz

55. Barro, John. "The Crisis in the Republican Party Is Even Worse than It Looks," *Business Insider*, May 3, 2016, accessed May 3, 2016, http://www.business insider.com/donald-trump-nomination-gop-crisis-2016-5

56. Thompson, Derek. "Trump vs. Clinton: A Battle between Two Opposite Americas," *The Atlantic*, April 28, 2016, accessed May 19, 2016, http://www.theatlantic.com/politics/archive/2016/04/clinton-trump/480162/

57. Hattem, Julian. "Trump Warns against 'False Song of Globalism,'" *The Hill*, April 27, 2016, accessed May 19, 2016, http://thehill.com/policy/national-security/277879-trump-warns-against-false-song-of-globalism

58. Ibid.

59. Merry, Robert W. "Trump vs. Hillary Is Nationalism vs. Globalism, 2016," *The National Interest*, May 4, 2016, accessed May 4, 2016, http://nationalinterest.org.mutex.gmu.edu/feature/trump-vs-hillary-nationalism-vs-globalism-2016–16041?page=2

60. Boersma, Tim, Charles K. Ebinger, and Heather Greenley. "The Presidential Candidates' Views on Energy and Climate," *Brookings*, June 9, 2016, accessed June 9, 2016, http://www.brookings.edu/blogs/order-from-chaos/posts/2016/06/09-candidates-energy-policy-boersma-ebinger-greenley?

utm_campaign=Brookings+Brief&utm_source=hs_email&utm_medium=email&
utm_content=30497484&_hsenc=p2ANqtz-8C8sIH7h9mlgYwQeRG-hlfruizI2LdCO
8qa6bjyD8VPrHcIm2_l_jrxlGCeu9LWioXfCbsFTDLNcsRyHWXJFmRUHNQkg&_
hsmi=30497484

61. Inside Gov Staff. "Candidate Comparison," *Inside Gov by Graphiq, accessed June 9, 2016, http://presidential-candidates.insidegov.com/compare/40–70/Hillary-Clinton-vs-Donald-Trump

62. Trump, Donald J. "Tax Reform That Will Make American Great Again: The Goals of Donald J. Trump's Tax Plan," *Trump: Make American Great Again!* Accessed June 15, 2016, https://www.donaldjtrump.com/positions/tax-reform

63. Clinton, Hillary. "Every American Should be Able to Learn the Skills They Need to Compete and Succeed," *Hillary Clinton*, accessed June 18, 2016, https://www. hillaryclinton.com/issues/workforce-and-skills/

64. Rees, Alex. "What 18 Former Apprentice Candidates Really Think of Donald Trump," *Cosmopolitan*, February 22, 2016, accessed June 19, 2016, http://www. cosmopolitan.com/entertainment/celebs/news/a53886/apprentice-candidates-on-donald-trump/

65. Ibid.

66. Ibid.

67. Ibid.

68. TIME Staff. "Here's Donald Trump's Presidential Announcement Speech," *TIME*, June 16, 2015, accessed June 9, 2016, http://time.com/3923128/donald-trump-announcement-speech/

69. Goldberg, Eleanor. "80% of Central American Women, Girls Are Raped Crossing into the U.S.," *Huffington Post*, September 12, 2014, accessed April 17, 2016, http://www.huffingtonpost.com/2014/09/12/central-america-migrants-rape_n_5806972.html

70. Trump, Donald J., and Tony Schwartz. *Trump: The Art of the Deal.* New York, NY: Ballantine Books, (2009): 56.

71. Confessore, Nicholas, and Karen Yourish, ""$2 Billion Worth of Free Media for Donald Trump,"" *New York Times*, March 15, 2016, accessed May 29, 2016, http:// www.nytimes.com/2016/03/16/upshot/measuring-donald-trumps-mammoth-advantage-in-free-media.html?_r=0

72. Smith, Allan. "Stunning Chart Shows How Donald Trump has Dominated Media Coverage of the 2016 Race," *Business Insider: UK*, March 15, 2016, accessed June 17, 2016, http://uk.businessinsider.com/donald-trump-media-coverage-chart-2016–3?r=US&IR=T

73. Lewis, Philip. "Donald Trump on Climate change: 'I Believe It Goes Up and It Goes Down," *The Huffington Post*, September 22, 2015, accessed June 18, 2016, http://www.huffingtonpost.com/entry/trump-global-warming_us_5601d04fe4b0 8820d91aa753

74. Guarino, Ben. "Donald Trump Calls Global Warming a Hoax—Until It Threatens His Golf Course," *Independent*, May 25, 2016, accessed May 25, 2016, http://www.independent.co.uk/environment/climate-change/donald-trump-called-global-warming-a-hoax-until-it-threatened-his-golf-course-a7047486. html

75. Trump, Donald J. "This very expensive GLOBAL WARMING bullshit has got to stop. Our planet is freezing, record low temps, and our GW scientists are stuck in ice," *Twitter*, January 1, 2014, accessed June 18, 2016, https://mobile.twitter. com/realDonaldTrump/status/418542137899491328

76. Trump. Donald J. "The concept of global warming was created by and for the Chinese in order to make U.S. manufacturing non-competitive," *Twitter*, November 6, 2012, accessed June 18, 2016, https://mobile.twitter.com/realDonaldTrump/status/265895292191248385
77. Schreckinger, Ben. "Donald Trump Acknowledges Climate Change—at His Irish Golf Course," *Politico*, May 23, 2016, accessed June 19, 2016, http://www.politico.eu/article/donald-trump-acknowledges-climate-change-at-his-irish-golf-course/

2   Win with Me

Defining National Identity

Each person has an individual way of describing him or herself and his or her interactions with the various groups he or she connects with. We want others to think of us as unique in terms of our own views, values, and positions. Although it is important for us to be considered as having a distinctive personality, it is also vital for us to belong to particular social groups.[1] This connection to groups—social identity—is an essential part of how we see ourselves and how we perceive society as a whole. Our social identity is based on the belief that, as individuals, we belong to a particular group; we share common views, values, and feelings with other group members; and we differ significantly from members of other social groups. This social group we belong to provides us with a particular social status, in addition to protection and security. Group membership also provides us with a clear set of shared ideas and values; it is where we obtain positive self-esteem and develop particular visions and understandings of other ethnic, religious, political, racial, or national groups.

In order to form an understanding about the nation to which they belong, people mirror the narratives of particular leaders.[2] They appropriate and render specific characteristics, values, and beliefs of these leaders in order to make meaning of society, inclusive of the political realm.[3] People's views regarding the nation and the political order are, thus, usually borrowed from the particular leader they identify with. In societies with many different and often competing national narratives, such as the U.S., this borrowing of ideas from a leader becomes a matter of choice for individuals.[4] The leaders who provide national narratives that resonate with a majority of the population can define the meaning of the nation and create a shared identity among their followers.

Accepting a person as a group leader, which entails supporting and displaying loyalty to this individual, depends on both the leader and his/her

supporters sharing a similar vision. Leaders who share similar views, grievances, and points of discontent are frequently perceived as supportive of
group goals, which has the result of making such individuals highly persuasive and influential.[5]

How did Donald Trump originally emerge as a leader? He has never held
public office at any level of government. Why after announcing his candidacy
for president on June 16, 2015, did he immediately gain strong popular support? Interestingly, this was not really something new for American politics.
In 2011, Trump had a nine-point lead in a national poll of the hypothetical
Republican presidential field: Trump was supported by 26 percent of likely
primary voters, followed by former Arkansas governor Mike Huckabee with
17 percent and former Massachusetts governor Mitt Romney with 15 percent.[6] Although Trump did not enter the race at the time, his hypothetical lead
was connected to the fact that he was much better known than the other candidates. As Conor Friedersdorf at the *Atlantic* wrote then, "Look at Donald
Trump. Yes, he's a national joke, but he's been given a lot more attention *as a
contender for the presidency* than a lot of folks who've served multiple terms
in the Senate or a statehouse."[7] Peter Hart, a Democratic pollster agreed:
"The voters know Trump; they do not know many of the others."[8] Success of
The Apprentice, a fourteen-season reality game show that assesses the business skills of competing contestants, has made Trump a household name in
the U.S. His words "You are fired!" had become to many symbolic of power,
strength, and success. The Trump name also adorns luxury condominiums,
hotels, and golf courses around the world. Through vigorous self-promotion,
his trademark has become a symbol for luxury and glamour. Trump receives
millions of dollars for simply putting the Trump name on companies owned
by other business owners. The value of his company's "deals, brand and
branded developments" is worth $3 billion, which makes his brand the most
significant holding in his portfolio.[9]

Moreover, the fact that Trump has led the debate over whether President
Obama is a U.S. citizen is another reason for Trump's notoriety. Trump started
the "birther" movement and hired a private investigator to go to Hawaii and
find out about Obama's birth certificate. Voters who have disapproved of
Obama's presidency liked or identified with Trump's "no-nonsense, take-no-
prisoners approach."[10] In addition, as people desperately wanted an upturn
in the current economic situation in the U.S. and, crucially, more jobs, they
have bought into the idea that, as a businessman, Trump will know how to
deliver nationwide economic prosperity.

Finally, many people perceive Trump to be particularly charismatic. As a
former *Apprentice* contestant stated, "He's attractive in person. It's probably
the sense of confidence and power," "Donald Trump walked in, he didn't say
anything [at first] but in that moment, you knew that he exuded power. He

dominated the space," "he is a really, really funny guy. He's very sharp, and he's very witty," "he is really personable [and] he puts you at ease. I felt very comfortable around him." "He's a big personality on and off screen."[11]

When Trump announced his candidacy in 2015, he already had a group of likely followers. Those who support Trump, for example, feel connected with the vision of America he has been promoting since the beginning of his campaign. As a result, they have revised their understanding of American society based on his descriptions. This similarity of views between Trump and his supporters is reflected in the importance placed on a certain conception of American national identity, feelings of economic stress and dissatisfaction with the current government, and negative perceptions of other national groups.

First, Trump has echoed the importance of a specific meaning of American national identity and has run his campaign on the idea of making "America great again." In America, the most important social identity for the majority of White people is being American. They do not have a stronger sense of ethnic identity, even if some recognize and cherish their ethnic heritage.[12] This feeling of importance associated with being an American is typically significantly stronger among Whites than it is among African Americans or Latinos.[13] For many White Americans, religious and national identities are also commonly connected. This conception of national identity is the one that gives them a sense of pride, affords meaning to social reality, and provides a set of ideas for assessing themselves and others. For the majority of Trump supporters, who describe their ancestry as American, this strong national identity is crucial.[14]

An understanding of what it means to be an American usually differs among people. Commonly accepted features of American national identity, among most, are an exclusive use of English, observance of American national holidays, and the use of American symbols.[15] Many also believe that two major components of American national identity comprise Anglo-Protestant heritage and "American creed" (egalitarianism, liberty, and individualism).[16]

The idea of American citizenship is at the center of Trump's campaign. Trump entered the presidential race challenging commonly accepted views of national identity. "Thanks to Trump, this has become a political contest about national identity, with the core question being, 'What sort of country is America?'"[17] Trump stresses his "Americanness" and his devotion to its prosperity. In Trump's *The America We Deserve*, he writes about the American Dream:

> That dream made it the best country in history. It's the dream my father and mother dreamed, the one they made come true for our family. It's the one that took me to the top. When you mess with the American Dream, you're on the fighting side of Trump.[18]

His favorite American symbol is the New York skyline, a picture that, for many people worldwide, represents America. For Trump, it is an emblem of strength, constant recovery, and success: "Whatever happens, it always come up a little brighter and a few stories higher . . . The lessons it teaches—lessons of hope, opportunity, struggle and accomplishment—can help support us through the good times and sustain us when the bad time come."[19] He has claimed restoring the American Dream will be at the heart of his presidency: "America first will be the major and overriding theme of my administration."[20] In another speech at a rally he noted, "What do we all want? We want a strong country."[21]

He has also continually sought to protect the interests of American citizens against those who he believes disparage citizenship. Trump views the Obama administration as putting America second in relation to international humanitarian values, the promotion of cosmopolitanism, and the transformation of the national economy into a globally competitive marketplace instead of defending the rights of U.S. citizens. Trump, in contrast, privileges the rights of Americans over a more universalist concept of rights. He specifically targets groups that do not have American citizenship: undocumented aliens, Syrian refugees, or Muslim immigrants trying to enter the U.S.

Trump lends credence to his supporters' belief that English should be the only language used in the U.S. by echoing such a sentiment: "We're a nation that speaks English. I think that, while we're in this nation, we should be speaking English. Whether people like it or not, that's how we assimilate."[22] According to his supporters, "Each issue with which he engages . . . is connected to American identity. No borders—no country. No money or jobs—no country. No unity—no country. No sovereignty—no country. Trump understands this, and he wants America to last for generations."[23]

Second, despite Trump's substantial wealth, he has managed to create a common identity with White working-class people. In his book *The America We Deserve*, Trump analyzed the success of Wendell Willkie, a Republican candidate who ran against Franklin Roosevelt. Trump noted, "Even though he was a millionaire businessman he had a way of relating to the common man. He criticized the platform of both Democrats and Republicans for 'double talk, weasel words and evasion.'"[24] He believes this approach can be successful in getting him the presidency:

> Most politicians use language to conceal what they think. Many are trained as lawyers and speak to win support rather than to define the truth. I use language to speak my mind. Being blunt hasn't hurt me so far. I've lived my life as I choose and said what I wanted to say.[25]

Trump has used this straightforward approach to address the feelings of economic and social deprivation among the American working class. Among

Trump supporters, 81 percent believed that international trade agreements promote unfair competition, which hurts the U.S., whereas only 60 percent of Cruz supporters agreed. Fifty-five percent of Trump supporters believed that free trade is damaging for the U.S. in comparison to 41 percent of Cruz supporters. And, finally, 37 percent of Trump supporters believed it is important to focus on domestic problems (twice as high in comparison with Cruz supporters).[26] A majority of people agree the U.S. economy is not in good shape. Former president Bill Clinton stated that President Barak Obama's description of the economy did not reflect the everyday experiences of Americans: "Millions of people look at that pretty picture of America he painted and they could not find themselves in it."[27]

A majority of Republicans view global economic involvement as not in the best interest of America, with Trump supporters being the most skeptical of U.S. involvement in the global economy.[28] Trump promises to punish corporations that outsource jobs and factories across the border to Mexico and further abroad, and he has promised to create government tax incentives to keep auto production in America and to limit the U.S. (auto) market to Japanese imports until the Japanese government drops trade barriers. Announcing his candidacy for president, Trump stated, "I'll bring back our jobs from China, from Mexico, from Japan, from so many places. I'll bring back our jobs, and I'll bring back our money."[29] During his rallies in different states, Trump has constantly returned to this issue. "We will keep the car industry in Michigan and we're going to bring car companies back to Michigan," he stated on the campaign trail.[30] Continuing to focus on addressing the profound problems with the car industry in the U.S., Trump stated,

> I don't like what's happening. We're losing our jobs. We're losing our wealth. We're losing our country . . . Why can't we do it in this country? It's an incredible thing that we're not allowed to make our product.[31]

Whereas many have been critical and have highlighted Trump's promises to be empty and unlikely to be come to fruition,[32] people are eager to believe in them and see Trump as their leader. Despite the fact that the majority of his proposed solutions seem unrealistic, they are easy to understand and support. As one supporter noted, "I do not believe in everything Trump proposes, but people want change, not a re-circulated Governor, Senator, and Vice President."[33]

Pertinently, people believe the current government is unable or unwilling to address these issues. Forty-seven percent of Trump supporters feel frustrated and "angry" at the federal government and 40 percent of them "feel betrayed by Republican politicians" (twice as high in comparison to Cruz supporters).[34] The last time the majority of Americans believed the country was on the "right track" was in 2003.[35] Neither party appears to have a clear solution for these problems. As a result, "rapid, disorienting economic and cultural change has led a substantial group of Americans to turn to someone who disdains feckless politicians and pledges to restore the country's strength."[36] As discussed in the introduction, Trump has actively stressed how different he is to the current American political elite who have only catered to the interests of wealthy donors. He promised a campaign independent of the influences of outside money:

> I will tell you that our system is broken. I gave to many people. Before this, before two months ago, I was a businessman. I give to everybody. When they call, I give. And you know what? When I need something from them, two years later, three years later, I call them. They are there for me. And that's a broken system.[37]

Trump has also echoed the dissatisfaction of his followers: "The country is fed up with what's going on. You know, in the old days they used the term 'silent majority'; we have the silent majority back, folks."[38] In his book *The America We Deserve*, Trump stated, the "American people want to be told the truth. They know we don't have the political leaders we deserve, and they know if the things don't change we won't have the America we deserve."[39] Responding to criticism from the Speaker of the House, Paul Ryan, Trump stated,

> Perhaps in the future we can work together and come to an agreement about what is best for the American people. They have been treated so badly for so long that it is about time for politicians to put them first![40]

This position strongly resonates with Trump followers. As one supporter noted, "He's for the working class and seems to be revealing a lot of things about the government we haven't known."[41] Another supporter echoed this sentiment, stating, "He might not be the smartest in the race, but he is going to bring back our jobs. He'll fight for us. He's a fighter."[42] Yet another supporter said, "He may be a jerk, but he's our jerk."[43] The leadership of Women Vote Trump stated, "He has the brains, drive and determination to be successful. He takes action, and gets things done in the real world."[44]

Third, to increase solidarity and loyalty, leaders tend to emphasize differences with other groups and engender antipathy toward them. This strategy is not alien to Trump: from his very first speech, when he announced his candidacy, he has strategically positioned people without American citizenship as enemies. He has described them as a threat to the economic well-being of the nation or as a "fifth column" that is seeking to destroy national prosperity.

The two groups most frequently targeted by Trump are illegal Mexican immigrants and Muslim immigrants. Building upon already established negative perceptions of illegal immigrants, Trump has manipulated these perceptions by echoing people's prejudices. During a debate inside Cleveland's Quicken Loans Arena, Trump made a point of stating,

> the Mexican government is much smarter, much sharper, much more cunning. They send the bad ones over, because they don't want to pay for them, they don't want to take care of them. Why should they, when the stupid leaders of the United States will do it for "me?"[45]

Trump has also proposed to build a wall that will run the length of the Mexico/U.S. border in order to stop illegal immigration. In his two-page memo to the *Washington Post*, he outlined his strategy, which consists of forcing Mexico to pay for a border wall. He has also threatened to stop the ways in which immigrants send money back to their families in Mexico.[46] Trump's official immigration plan places enormous emphasis on the cost of illegal immigration for U.S. taxpayers, particularly concerning the health-care, housing, education, and welfare costs brought about by illegal immigrants.

Trump's plan further emphasizes a connection between crime rates and illegal immigration, citing "cases of criminals who crossed our border illegally only to go on to commit horrific crimes against Americans."[47] Trump's plan has also connected illegal immigration to the low salaries and high unemployment rates among working-class Americans. As a solution, Trump has pledged to "impound all remittance payments from illegal wages,"[48] to hike fees on temporary visas and border-crossing cards, to enforce criminal penalties for overstaying visas, and to end birthright citizenship for children of illegal immigrants.

People who think that illegal immigration is a profound issue facing the U.S. are among the strongest supporters of candidate Donald Trump.[49] Sixty percent of people who believe illegal immigrants threaten American customs and values favor Trump over any other candidate.[50] They believe the nation's changing demographics "represent a decline of America and American values and norms."[51] As one supporter stated, "Many policemen and firefighters are voting Trump because of immigrants getting jobs." Another supporter mentioned that Trump's immigration policy was a big reason she was attracted to him: "Why should people sneak in?"[52] Another supporter echoed this sentiment, stating, "That he's going to send them packing."[53] The need for a wall is one of the first things people mention when asked to explain their support for Trump, and they collectively chant, "Build That Wall!" during his rallies.[54]

Trump has also received support from some legal Hispanic immigrants and citizens. One member of the organization Latinos for the Wall stated, "I'm just tired of paying for the freeloaders."[55] Support for Trump increased when protesters in California were waiving Mexican flags while they set the American flag on fire. As one Trump supporter stated,

> Brandishing Mexican flags and burning American flags sends a clear message as to which national identity the demonstrators prefer . . . It portends to a future where millions of young people think of America with contempt as they cling to their native land and culture.[56]

In their letter endorsing Trump, American Border Patrol Agents stated,

> If we do not secure our borders, American communities will continue to suffer at the hands of gangs, cartels and violent criminals preying on the innocent . . . In view of these threats, the National Border Patrol Council endorses Donald J. Trump for President—and asks the American people to support Mr. Trump in his mission to finally secure the border of the United States of America, before it is too late.[57]

Trump has also targeted Muslim immigrants, echoing the belief prevalent among his supporters that they are a threat to America. Republicans who believe Muslims pose an immediate threat to the U.S. are more supportive of Trump than Republicans who think Muslims are not a threat to the country. Similarly, GOP primary voters who said most Muslims support ISIS are significantly more likely to support Trump than Republicans who think "very few" adherents of Islam support the terrorist organization.[58]

Trump has proposed a radical change in how the government should approach the issue of Muslim immigrants: "We're going to have to do things that we never did before," Trump said. "And some people are going to be upset about it, but I think that now everybody is feeling that security is going to rule. And certain things will be done that we never thought would happen in this country in terms of information and learning about the enemy. And so we're going to have to do certain things that were frankly unthinkable a year ago."[59] When Trump was asked whether there should be a database to track Muslims, he replied: "There should be a lot of systems, beyond databases. We should have a lot of systems."[60] Although Trump pointed out the idea of a database of names had come from a journalist, he did not denounce it, but rather reiterated the importance of a watch list. He defended his position by referring to former president Roosevelt's 1942 executive order to deport 110,000 American citizens of Japanese descent: "This is a president highly respected by all, he did the same thing. If you look at what he was doing, it was far worse. We are now at war. We have a president that doesn't want to say that, but we are now at war."[61] As evidenced by this comment, Trump did not disavow the deportation of Japanese Americans, noting it should be judged from the historic perspective. This position strongly resonates with his followers. As one supporter stated, "I'm for Trump because he talks about Muslims the way we talk about Muslims."[62]

The levels of agreement and engagement with Trump may vary among supporters, but their personal accounts of the nation in a majority of cases reflect the ideas expressed by Trump. This similarity with Trump's views and positions about America provides his supporters with their meaning of national identity, their connection to the nation, and temporal coherence. It helps his supporters to clearly define who "we" are and who are the "other," in addition to their real or perceived rights, grievances, and positions within the nation.

In a situation of crisis or uncertainty, people leave decision making to the group and its leadership. Seeing similarities between their beliefs and positions with those of Trump, people accept him as a leader and join the group of his supporters, assuming the supporters are like them.[63] They feel at ease and comfortable in this new group because it promotes ideas in line with their beliefs and values.[64] They also feel more satisfied, as they lend more weight to the views that support their beliefs, while discarding contradictory information, regardless of how factual it may be. Finally, they feel more confident: agreement with Trump's rhetoric and actions and with his supporters satisfies their desire to be right as a group and to avoid embarrassment by being accused of aggressive or intolerant views.

Trump supporters, therefore, find confirmation for their existing biases and perceptions in his speeches, which, in turn, increases their connection to him. Many Trump supporters reject the notion that their views are intolerant or racist.

> These people were actually surprised. They said, "Why would you think we're racist because we want to protect America? When Muslim terrorists want to come into America and blow up our buildings and kill us, why is keeping Muslims out racist?"[65]

His supporters even accept new attitudes that go beyond their usual perceptions and beliefs. Moreover, they start to see themselves as agents of his will, carrying out his wishes as their own, and they lay all responsibility for their actions with Trump. Trump, thus, feeds on obedience, as people come to view themselves as the instrument of their leader's will.[66]

Increasing Self-Esteem of Voters

Trump's rhetoric about Hispanic and Muslim immigrants not only resonates with the prejudices of his supporters but also simultaneously increases their self-esteem. People have a strong need for a positive identity. It is important for us to feel good about ourselves and about our actions, as well as to know that other people like us exist, and they view us positively. People with high self-esteem feel happier and more self-assured. But how can people acquire high self-esteem? This is typically achieved when we feel good about ourselves and other people appreciate our achievements, our good deeds, and our personal characteristics. But unfortunately, this is often not enough for many people, and they search for other sources of positive self-worth. The easiest way to obtain this is by comparing ourselves favorably to other people or groups, whereby we describe them in a negative light. Viewing others as less educated, impolite, and irresponsible, among other things, helps us feel better about ourselves and increases our positive outlook.[67] When people see themselves as better than others, their self-esteem receives a significant boost.

Members of groups from lower social and economic social positions have fewer prospects to see themselves positively based on their successes or place in society. They feel less satisfied and secure, and they display less positive social identity than members of more advantaged groups.[68] The majority of blue-collar Whites in the U.S. do not have opportunities to make their identity more positive and, therefore, have a strong need to compare themselves with members of other groups and, in turn, put these groups down in the process. They increase their self-esteem by emphasizing the negative aspects and characteristics of other groups.[69]

Trump has helped his supporters use this comparison with other groups by emphasizing the differences between them.[70] Negative descriptions of Hispanics and Muslims create a feeling, among his supporters, that they are better than members of these groups, which helps to increase their self-esteem significantly. Their prejudices and biases are not based on the need to discriminate against others, but rather come from a need for the feeling of self-worth and, thus, favorable comparison with others. The more people need high self-esteem, the more they appear to display discrimination against others. Trump followers are supporting his prejudicial positions because by doing so they are able to see themselves in a better light.

By building upon shared values and ideas, in addition to perceptions of himself as prototypical, Trump has been able to position himself as a prototype among his supporters. To raise his legitimacy, Trump has not only become a representative of this identity but has also championed the interests of this group, formed an in-group identity, and shaped reality in the image of this in-group identity. His legitimacy as a leader gives him the right to prescribe appropriate beliefs, attitudes, or behavior in certain areas.[71] His supporters happily agree they ought to follow him. They have endowed him with the power to express their collective will and define the right course of action.[72] In turn, he seemingly encourages his supporters to achieve their goals, which have at their core the creation of a particular social order.

For example, Trump supporters feel their biases against Muslims and Hispanics are justified. One of two brothers from South Boston who were arrested for beating a fifty-eight-year-old man with a metal pole told police, "Donald Trump was right, all these illegals need to be deported."[73] Another man who attacked Muslim and Hispanic students near the Wichita State campus shouted, "Brown trash, go home. Trump will win." After kicking one student, he circled around them on a monocycle saying, "Trump, Trump, Trump, we will make America great again. You losers will be thrown out of the wall."[74]

Empowering Supporters

The identity Trump has created also empowers his followers. When people feel unsatisfied with national policies and their economic and social situation, connecting with a leader can inspire people to promote their view of the nation and its future, inclusive of actively demanding change.[75] In this process of "social becoming," supporters become more empowered and believe their leader will give them an opportunity to redefine the meaning of national identity. Trump emphasizes the idea of a common identity that empowers people: "This is a movement. I don't want it to be about me. This is about common sense. It's about doing the right thing."[76] Through Trump, his supporters hope to attain more power and authority, take control of their own lives, and actively participate in shaping the vision of the nation. Trump supporters feel more empowered through participation in rallies, their involvement in his campaign, and by forming connections with other supporters.[77]

Trump supporters believe Trump will give them the power required to deal with their national and local problems and to restore the strength of the American neglected working class. The majority of his supporters feel powerless and voiceless, believing "people like me don't have any say about what the government does."[78] They want to have a say in their own country. They think the current establishment has no willingness to change or compromise; they trust that Trump will be able to undermine the confidence that other people continue to show toward the current political establishment in power and, thus, will bring his supporters to a long-standing victory.[79] As one supporter stated,

> I lived in a once great country where the air and water are now poisoned . . . and poor children can't have decent education. I support Trump because

he makes other politicians feel the way they make me feel: angry, frustrated, and hopeless.[80]

Another supporter agreed: "He's not bought and paid for. He says it the way it is. He's not afraid to offend anybody."[81] His independence from mainstream politics is very important for Trump supporters:

I'm totally behind Donald Trump because he's not a politician. He's not a Washington bureaucrat; he doesn't come out of Obama's sneaky White House. He's clean, and he's free. He doesn't need this; he's one of the wealthiest men in the country, but he sees what's going on in the country and he wants to save it.[82]

Trump supporters also feel he has been creating a degree of uncertainty among the established political elite by challenging their politically expedient ways of running the country. This, in turn, gives more power to Trump and his supporters. As one of his supporters stated, "I love Donald Trump because he's totally politically incorrect. He's gone after every group."[83] Another supporter echoed this sentiment by noting that "he's saying the things no one else says."[84] Yet another supporter emphasized Trump's courage: "He's not afraid to say what everybody's feeling and afraid to say. He doesn't have a filter."[85]

In this process of empowerment, Trump simultaneously promotes his ideas among his followers and challenges existing power structures. He helps his supporters to gain more awareness of their situation and believe they can change it. This change can be supported through different meanings but the confrontational attitude Trump promotes makes the use of force an option in order to achieve their desired goals. In his view, aggression makes sense and helps to involve those who are on the margins of mainstream political debates and who do not believe in the force of debate. They see themselves as social and political underdogs.[86] As one supporter stated, "I like Donald Trump because we're weak," he said. "I think we need a tough leader"[87]

Trump has artfully connected the frustrations of his supporters, their aggression, and their love for the U.S. For him, the violence of angry people is justifiable because they are fighting for their vision of the country. Responding to the incident when a seventy-eight-year-old Trump supporter punched a twenty-six-year-old protester, Trump stated,

You're mentioning one case—which I haven't seen, I heard about it—which I don't like. But when they see what's going on in this country, they have anger that's unbelievable. They have anger. They love this country. They don't like seeing bad trade deals, they don't like seeing higher taxes, they don't like seeing a loss of their jobs where our jobs have just been devastated. And I know—I mean, I see it. There is some anger. There's also great love for the country. It's a beautiful thing in many respects. But I certainly do not condone that at all.[88]

Similarly, one of two brothers from South Boston who were arrested for beating a fifty-eight-year-old Hispanic man told police "Donald Trump was right, all these illegals need to be deported." When asked about this incident, Trump said, "I will say that people who are following me are very passionate. They love this country and they want this country to be great again. They are passionate."[89] The idea that violence can be a response to economic grievances and cultural stress has empowered Trump supporters and given them the necessary reassurance that their passion and love of country is "a beautiful thing." However, after being challenged by journalists, Trump finally tweeted, "Boston incident is terrible. We need energy and passion, but we must treat each other with respect. I would never condone violence."[90]

The strategy Trump employs to empower his supporters is clearly described, ironically, by Saul Alinsky an American activist from the 1960s–1970s who has worked on improving conditions in African American ghettos in Chicago:

> The organizer . . . must first rub raw the resentments of the people in the community; fan the latent hostility of many of the people to the point of overt expression . . . An organizer must stir up dissatisfaction and discontent; provide a channel into which people can angrily pour their frustrations. He [sic] must create a mechanism that can drain off the underlying guilt for having accepted the previous situation for so long.[91]

Similarly, Trump has ignited the dissatisfaction of his followers, but has also provided an outlet for their dissatisfaction and frustration by defining "scapegoat" groups and blaming the existing political leadership in the U.S. Moreover, his followers appreciate his aggressive demeanor. As Alinsky stated, "A good tactic is one your people enjoy."[92] Trump leverages this readiness for violence among his supporters. He stated if he wasn't nominated at the Republican Convention in July, "I think you'd have riots. I think you'd have riots. You know, I'm representing a tremendous—many, many millions of people, in many cases first time voters."[93]

Trump also actively utilizes several of Alinsky's rules: "Wherever possible go outside the experience of the enemy" and "The major premise for tactics is the development of operations that will maintain constant pressure upon the opposition. It is this that will cause the opposition to react to your advantage."[94] Trump repeats the same insults over and over again, cementing them in the minds of people. For example, he emphasized a connection between the Clintons and the notion of deceit. Speaking about Bill Clinton during an interview, Trump stated, "He lied about it. He said, nothing happened with Monica Lewinsky, and then he said, sorry folks, it actually did happen." He immediately connected this idea of being dishonest to Hillary Clinton:

> She spoke a few weeks ago and she said, I'm going to put the miners and the companies out of business. Then she went to West Virginia and she tried to pretend she didn't make the statement, and that's the way it is with her. The lies and the deception, it's horrible.[95]

He also tweeted, "Crooked Hillary Clinton, perhaps the most dishonest person to have ever run for the presidency, is also one of the all time great enablers!"[96] Referring to the e-mail scandal[97] that has surrounded Hilary Clinton while serving as secretary of state, Trump stated, "She should not be allowed to run in the election. She should suffer like other people have suffered who have done far less than she has."[98] These attacks on Clinton contribute to the increasing perception among some of the American electorate who describe Hilary Clinton as "dishonest," a "liar," that they "don't trust her" and that she has a "poor character."[99]

Promising a Victory

The overarching idea Trump has placed at the center of the common identity he shares with his supporters is that of winning. Trump actively promotes his image as a winner: "I am a winner. If I am elected I will make this country a total winner—I will Make America Great Again";[100] "we will have so much winning if I get elected that you may get bored with the winning."[101] The self-presentation of Trump as a winner not only provides a degree of hope to his supporters but also creates positive connections with this identity. In his statements, Trump unites his supporters with his winning image. He uses "we" and gives this "we-ness" the power of change: "We've got ourselves a movement. It's a movement toward making America great again";[102] "we are going to do something so good and so fast and so strong. And the world is going to respect us again . . . We are going to start winning again."[103]

He understands that people love to be associated with a winner because it gives them positive self-esteem and a feeling of self-importance. In his book, he describes such a strategy:

> The final key to the way I promote is bravado. I play to people's fantasies. People may not always think big themselves, but they can still get very excited by those who do. That's why a little hyperbole never hurts. People want to believe that something is the biggest and the greatest and the most spectacular.[104]

By emulating this, Trump created identity; people connect themselves with the very idea of winning and success, which helps them to position themselves as victors. They feel empowered through their association with a successful business mogul and their common, shared identity. As one of his supporter stated, "Trump is the big time, the bright lights, the fancy everything— and wealth and fame and all things I am not but would like to be."[105] Another supporter echoed this sentiment: "I have a great amount of interest and respect to anyone that can grow a business with that many people—a wild amount of respect."[106] Yet, another supporter stated, Donald Trump has created the us-versus-them story, the winner-versus-loser story. And people always want to be [aligned] with the winner."[107]

The instruments Trump uses to create this common social identity and empower people include favorable comparison and exclusion, insults, and bullying. The next chapter will explore how people interpret this behavior as a demonstration of Trump's strength, which, enables them to empower themselves through their connection to him as a formidable leader.

Notes

1. Tajfel, Henri, and John C. Turner. "The Social Identity Theory of Intergroup Behaviour," *in Psychology of Intergroup Relations*, ed. Stephen Worchel and William G. Austin, 2nd ed. Chicago: Nelson-Hall, 1985: 7–24; Tajfel, Henri, ed. *Differentiation Between Social Groups: Studies in the Social Psychology of Intergroup Relations.* Academic Press, 1979.
2. Greenwalt, Kyle. "Discourse, Narrative, and National Identity: The Case of France." *Harvard Educational Review* 79, no. 3 (2009): 494–520; Hammack, Phillip L. *Narrative and the Politics of Identity: The Cultural Psychology of Israeli and Palestinian Youth*, 1st ed. Oxford, USA: Oxford University Press, 2010.
3. Hammack, Phillip L., and Andrew Pilecki. "Narrative as a root metaphor for political psychology." *Political Psychology* 33, no. 1 (2012): 75–103; Moghaddam, Fathali M. "The psychological citizen and the two concepts of social contract: A preliminary analysis." *Political Psychology* 29, no. 6 (2008): 881–901.
4. Habermas, J. "Citizenship and National Identity," in *Between Facts and Norms: Contributions to a Discourse Theory of Law and Democracy.* Cambridge: MIT Press, 1998.
5. Wenzel, Michael, and Prita Jobling, "Legitimacy of regulatory authorities as a function of inclusive identification and power over ingroups and outgroups." *European Journal of Social Psychology* 36, no. 2 (2006): 239–258.
6. Shahid, Aliyah. "Poll: Donald Trump Leads 2012 GOP Field: A New Poll Shows Trump Leading Huckabee, Romney, Gingrich, Palin, and Others," *US NEWS*, April 15, 2011, accessed April 18, 2016 http://www.usnews.com/news/articles/2011/04/15/poll-donald-trump-leads-2012-gop-field
7. James, Frank. "Donald Trump, Birther in Chief? Poll Has Him Leading GOP Field With 26 Percent," *NPR*, April 15, 2011, accessed April 16, 2016, http://www.npr.org/sections/itsallpolitics/2011/04/15/135446314/poll-donald-trump-birther-darling-leads-gop-field-at-26

44 *Win with Me*

8. Cillizza, Chris, and Aaron Blake. "Donald Trump: Seriously," *The Washington Post*, April 7, 2011, accessed April 10, 2016, https://www.washingtonpost.com/blogs/the-fix/post/donald-trump-seriously/2011/04/06/AF0481rC_blog.html
9. Johnson, Will, and Michael D'Antonio. "Trump's Campaign is Damaging His Brand," *Politico*, accessed April 12, 2016, http://www.politico.com/magazine/story/2016/01/donald-trump-2016-brand-business-213515
10. Cillizza, and Blake. "Donald Trump. Seriously."
11. Rees, "What 18 Former *Apprentice* Candidates Really Think of Donald Trump."
12. Bush, M. *Breaking the Code of Good Intention: Everyday Forms of Whiteness.* New York: Rowman & Littlefield, 2005; DeVos, T., & Banaji, M. R. "American = White?" *Journal of Personality and Social Psychology*, 88, (2005): 447–466.
13. Rodriguez, Liliana, Seth J. Schwartz, and Susan Krauss Whitbourne. "American identity revisited: The relation between national, ethnic, and personal identity in a multiethnic sample of emerging adults." *Journal of Adolescent Research*, 25, no. 2 (2010): 324–349.
14. Irwin, Neil, and Josh Katz. "The Geography of Trumpism," *New York Times*, March 13, 2016, accessed April 9, 2016, http://www.nytimes.com/2016/03/13/upshot/the-geography-of-trumpism.html?_r=0
15. Bush, M. *Breaking the Code of Good Intention: Everyday Forms of Whiteness.* New York: Rowman & Littlefield, 2005.
16. Huntington, Samuel P. *Who Are We?: The Challenges to America's National Identity*. Simon and Schuster. 2004.
17. Heer, Jeet. "Is America a Nation of Xenophobic Trumps," *New Republic*, November 20, 2015, accessed (date) Trumps"https://newrepublic.com/article/124295/america-nation-xenophobic-trumps
18. Trump, Donald. *The America We Deserve*. Macmillan, 2000.
19. Ibid.
20. Trump. Donald J. ""Foreign Policy," *Trump: Make America Great Again!* April 27, 2016, accessed May 1, 2016, https://www.donaldjtrump.com/press-releases/donald-j.-trump-foreign-policy-speech
21. Bouie, Jamie. "How Trump Happened," *Slate*, March 13, 2016, accessed April 18, 2016, http://www.slate.com/articles/news_and_politics/cover_story/2016/03/how_donald_trump_happened_racism_against_barack_obama.html
22. THR Staff. "Donald Trump: 'While We're in This Nation, We Should Be Speaking English,'" *The Hollywood Reporter*, September 3, 2015, accessed April 14, 2016, http://www.hollywoodreporter.com/news/donald-trump-speak-english-spanish-820215
23. Kane, Marie M. "Trump and the America identity," *American Thinker*, February 1, 2016, accessed April 10, 2016, http://www.americanthinker.com/blog/2016/02/trump_and_the_american_identity.html
24. Trump, Donald. *The America We Deserve*. Macmillan, 2000.
25. Ibid.
26. Wolfe, Julia, Randy Yeip, and Aaron Zitner. "How Trump Happened," *The Wall Street Journal*, 2016, accessed April 12, 2016, http://graphics.wsj.com/elections/2016/how-trump-happened/
27. Rhodan, Maya. "Bill Clinton Says Obama Painted a 'Pretty Picture' of the U.S.," *Time*, March 21, 2016, accessed April 10, 2016, http://time.com/4250018/bill-clinton-obama-america-dream/
28. Pew Research Center Staff. "Public Uncertain, Divided Over American' Place in the World."

29. Washington Post Staff. "Full text: Donald Trump announces a presidential bid."
30. Kessler, Glenn. "Trump's Trade Rhetoric, Stuck in a Time Warp," *The Washington Post*, March 18, 2016, accessed April 1, 2016, https://www.washingtonpost.com/news/fact-checker/wp/2016/03/18/trumps-trade-rhetoric-stuck-in-a-time-warp/
31. Shepardson, David. "Trump Suggests Moving Some Car Production from Michigan," *Detroit News Washington Bureau*, August 12, 2015, accessed April 2, 2016, http://www.detroitnews.com/story/business/autos/2015/08/12/trump-autos/31589899/
32. Kessler, "Trump's trade rhetoric, stuck in a time warp."
33. Von Drehle, David. "Destination Unknown," *Time*, March 14, 2016.
34. Malone, Clare. "Why Donald Trump? A Quest to Figure Out What's Happening in America," *FiveThirtyEight*, March 23, 2016, accessed April 1, 2016, http://fivethirtyeight.com/features/why-donald-trump/
35. Klein, Joe. "In the Arena," *TIME*, January 18, 2016 issue.
36. Bouie. "How Trump Happened."
37. Prokop, Andrew. "Donald Trump Made One Shockingly Insightful Comment during the First GOP Debate," *Vox*, August 6, 2015, accessed April 2, 2016, http://www.vox.com/2015/8/6/9114565/donald-trump-debate-money
38. Schwartz, Ian. "Trump: 'The Silent Majority Is Back,'" *RealClear Politics*, July 6, 2016, accessed July 6, 2016, http://www.realclearpolitics.com/video/2015/07/06/trump_the_silent_majority_is_back.html
39. Trump, Donald. *The America We Deserve*.
40. Bradner, Eric. "The GOP Resistance to Donald Trump," *CNN*, May 6, 2016, accessed May 17, 2016, http://www.cnn.com/2016/05/05/politics/paul-ryan-donald-trump-republican-resistance/
41. Malone, Clare. "Why Donald Trump? A Quest to Figure Out What's Happening in America," *FiveThirtyEight*, March 23, 2016, accessed April 1, 2016, http://fivethirtyeight.com/features/why-donald-trump/
42. Elliot, Phill. "Why Would Democrats Vote for Trump? It's All About Trade: The Unionized Heartland Is Focused on Jobs," *Times*, March 21, 2016.
43. Reich, Robert. "Why Trump Might Win," *Real Clear Politics*, May 24, 2016, accessed April 3, 2016, http://www.realclearpolitics.com/articles/2016/05/24/why_trump_might_win_130653.html
44. Accessed June 28, 2016, http://womenvotetrump.com
45. O'Reilly, Andrew. "At GOP Debate, Trump Says 'Stupid' U.S. Leaders Are Being Duped by Mexico," *Fox News Latino*, August 6, 2015, accessed April 3, 2016, http://latino.foxnews.com/latino/politics/2015/08/06/at-republican-debate-trump-says-mexico-is-sending-criminals-because-us/
46. Woodward, Bob and Robert Costa. "Trump Reveals How He would Force Mexico to Pay for Border Wall," *The Washington Post*, April 5, 2016, accessed April 3, 2016, https://www.washingtonpost.com/politics/trump-would-seek-to-block-money-transfers-to-force-mexico-to-fund-border-wall/2016/04/05/c0196314-fa7c-11e5-80e4-c381214de1a3_story.html
47. Trump, Donald J. "Immigration Reform That Will Make American Great Again: The Three Core Principles of Donald J. Trump's Immigration Plan," *Trump: Make America Great Again!* accessed May 19, 2016, https://www.donaldjtrump.com/positions/immigration-reform
48. Ibid.
49. Tesler, Michael. "How Anti-Immigrant Attitudes Are Fueling Support for Donald Trump," *The Washington Post*, November 24, 2015, accessed April 4, 2016,

https://www.washingtonpost.com/news/monkey-cage/wp/2015/11/24/
how-anti-immigrant-attitudes-are-fueling-support-for-donald-trump/
50. Pollard, Michael, and Joshua Mendelsohn. "RAND Kicks Off 2016 Presidential
    Election Panel Survey," *RAND Corporation*, January 27, 2016, accessed April 3,
    2016, https://www.rand.org/blog/2016/01/rand-kicks-off-2016-presidential-
    election-panel-survey.html
51. Bush, Daniel. "Could Trump's Anti-Muslim Rhetoric Influence Poli-
    tics Well beyond 2016?" *PBS Newshour*, December 11, 2015, accessed
    April 2, 2016, http://www.pbs.org/newshour/updates/could-trumps-anti-muslim-
    rhetoric-influence-politics-well-beyond-2016/
52. Malone, Clare. "Why Donald Trump? A Quest to Figure Out What's Happening
    in America," *FiveThirtyEight*, March 23, 2016, accessed April 1, 2016, http://
    fivethirtyeight.com/features/why-donald-trump/
53. Schreckinger, Ben. "Trump, Alabama and the Ghost of George Wallace,"
    Politico, August 21, 2015, accessed April 2, 2016, http://www.politico.com/
    story/2015/08/donald-trump-2016-mobile-alabama-rally-ghost-george-wallace-
    121627#ixzz3jkOWPAR1
54. Foss, Sarah. "Supporters See Trump, Sanders as Winners," *The Daily Gazette*,
    April 11, 2016, accessed April 11, 2016, http://www.dailygazette.com/weblogs/
    foss/2016/apr/11/0411_foss/http://www.dailygazette.com/weblogs/foss/2016/
    apr/11/0411_foss/
55. Kinney, Aaron, Bruce Newman, and Lindzi Wessel. "Donald Trump's Bizarre
    California GOP Convention Entrance Was Like 'crossing the border,'"
    The Mercury News, April 29, 2016, accessed April 30, 2016, http://www.
    mercurynews.com/politics-government/ci_29829794/trump-speech-
    today-kick-off-gop-convention-burlingame
56. Greer, Scott. "Anti-Trump Protesters Show Their True Colors With Mexican
    Flags," *Daily Caller*, May 1, 2016, accessed May 2, 2016, http://dailycaller.
    com/2016/05/01/anti-trump-protesters-show-their-true-colors-with-mexican-
    flags/#ixzz47Y07SRos
57. American's Border Patrol Agents. "America's Border Patrol Agents Issue
    Historic Letter of Endorsement for Donald J. Trump," *Trump: Make
    America Great Again!* March 30, 2016, accessed April 3, 2016, https://www.
    donaldjtrump.com/press-releases/americas-border-patrol-agentsissue-historic-
    letter-of-endorsement-for-donal
58. Tesler, Michael. "How Hostile Are Trump Supporters Toward Muslims? This New
    Poll Will Tell You," *The Washington Post*, December 8, 2016, accessed April 4,
    2016, https://www.washingtonpost.com/news/monkey-cage/wp/2015/12/08/
    how-hostile-are-trump-supporters-toward-muslims-this-new-poll-will-tell-you/
59. Heer, Jeet. "Is America a Nation of Xenophobic Trumps? *New Republic*, Novem-
    ber 20, 2015, accessed April 4, 2016, https://newrepublic.com/article/124295/
    america-nation-xenophobic-trumps
60. Graham, David A. "Is Donald Trump Serious about Registering Muslims?"
    The Atlantic, November 20, 2015, accessed April 4, 2016, http://www.theatlantic.
    com/politics/archive/2015/11/donald-trump-doubles-down-on-registering-
    muslims/416973/
61. Kaplan, Rebecca. "Trump Defends Muslim Plan by Comparing Himself to FDR,"
    CBSNews, December 8, 2015, accessed April 4, 2016, http://www.cbsnews.com/
    news/donald-trump-defends-muslim-plan-by-comparing-himself-to-fdr/

62. Klein, Joe. "Finding Moments of Republican Grace Amid the Ugly Bluster of Donald Trump," *Time*, February 11, 2016, accessed April 2, 2016, http://time.com/4217050/finding-moments-of-republican-grace-amid-the-ugly-bluster-of-donald-trump/
63. Asch, S. E. "Forming impressions of personality." *Journal of Abnormal and Social Psychology*, 41, (1946): 258–290.
64. Weiner, B. *An Attributional Theory of Motivation and Emotion*. New York: Springer-Verlag, 1986.
65. Malone, "Why Donald Trump?"
66. Milgram, Stanley. *Obedience to Authority: An Experimental View*. Harpercollins, 1974.
67. Tajfel, Henri, and John C. Turner. "The Social Identity Theory of Intergroup Behaviour," in *Psychology of Intergroup Relations*, ed. Stephen Worchel and William G. Austin, 2nd ed. Chicago: Nelson-Hall, (1985): 7–24.
68. Blanz, M., Mummendey, A., and Otten, S. "Perceptions of relative group size and group status: Effects on intergroup discrimination in negative evaluations," in *European Journal of Social Psychology*, 25, (1995): 231–247; Leonardelli, G. J., and Brewer, M. B. "Minority and majority discrimination: When and why?" in *Journal of Experimental Social Psychology* 37, (2001): 468–485.
69. Simon, B., Aufderheide, B., and Kampmeier, C. "The Social Psychology of Minority—Majority Relations," in *Blackwell Handbook of Social Psychology: Intergroup processes*, eds. R. Brown, and S. L. Gaertner. Oxford: Blackwell, (2001): 303–323.
70. Turner, J. C., Hogg, M. A., Oakes, P. J., Reicher, S. D., and Wetherell, M. S. *Rediscovering the Social Group: A Self-Categorization Theory*. Cambridge, MA, US: Basil Blackwell, (1987): 50.
71. Haslam, S. Alexander, Penelope J. Oakes, Katherine J. Reynolds, and John C. Turner. "Social identity salience and the emergence of stereotype consensus." *Personality and Social Psychology Bulletin* 25, no. 7 (1999): 809–818.
72. Turner, John C. "Explaining the nature of power: A three-process theory." *European Journal of Social Psychology* 35, no. 1 (2005): 1–22.
73. Rappeport, Allan. "A Beating in Boston said to be Inspired by Donald Trump's Immigration Comments," *New York Times*, August 20, 2015, accessed April 5, 2016, http://www.nytimes.com/politics/first-draft/2015/08/20/a-beating-in-boston-said-to-be-inspired-by-donald-trumps-immigrant-comments/
74. Morrison, Oliver. "Muslim Student at Wichita State Reports Attack by Man Shouting 'Trump, Trump, Trump,'" *The Wichita Eagle*, March 14, 2016, accessed April 2, 2016, http://www.kansas.com/news/local/crime/article65903602.html#storylink=cpy
75. E. A. Tiryakian. "Collective effervescence, social science and charism: Durkheim, Weber, and 1989." *International Sociology* 10, no. 3 (1995): 269–281.
76. Schreckinger, Ben. "Donald Trump: 'This is a movement,'" *Politico*, August 29, 2015, accessed April 3, 2016, http://www.politico.com/story/2015/08/donald-trump-2016-movement-213160#ixzz4AuDjj3Vm
77. Avruch, Kevin. *Context and Pretext in Conflict Resolution: Culture, Identity, Power, and Practice*. Routledge, 2015.
78. Thompson, Derek. "Who Are Donald Trump's Supporters, Really?" *The Atlantic*, March 1, 2016, accessed April 3, 2016, http://www.theatlantic.com/politics/archive/2016/03/who-are-donald-trumps-supporters-really/471714/
79. Curle, A. *Making Peace*. London: Tavistock, 1971.
80. March 21, 2016 issue of *Time*

81. Kinney, Aaron, Bruce Newman, and Lindzi Wessel, "Donald Trump's Bizarre California GOP Convention Entrance was Like 'Crossing the Border,'" *The Mercury News*, April 29, 2016, accessed June 1, 2016, http://www.mercurynews.com/politics-government/ci_29829794/trump-speech-today-kick-off-gop-convention-burlingame

82. Taylor, Jessica. "Why Trump Is Here to Stay—At Least for a While," *NPR*, August 21, 2015, accessed April 2, 2016, http://www.npr.org/sections/itsallpolitics/2015/08/21/433263471/trump-is-here-to-stay-at-least-for-a-while-heres-why

83. Catrett, Victoria. "Donald Trump's Art of the Steal," *Time*, January 18, 2016.

84. February 22, 2016 issue of *Time*.

85. Taylor, "Why Trump Is Here to Stay"

86. Groom, A. J. R., and K. Webb. "Injustice, empowerment and facilitation in conflict." *International Interactions* 13, no.3, (1987): 263–280.

87. Malone, "Why Donald Trump?"

88. CNN. "Transcript of Republican Debate in Miami, full Text," *CNN*, March 15, 2016, accessed April 4, 2016, http://www.cnn.com/2016/03/10/politics/republican-debate-transcript-full-text/

89. Rappeport, Allan. "A Beating in Boston Said to Be Inspired by Donald Trump's Immigration Comments," *New York Times*, August 20, 2015, accessed April 5, 2016, http://www.nytimes.com/politics/first-draft/2015/08/20/a-beating-in-boston-said-to-be-inspired-by-donald-trumps-immigrant-comments/

90. Trump, Donald J. "Boston incident is terrible: We need energy and passion, but we must treat each other with respect. I would never condone violence," *Twitter*, August 21, 2015, accessed April 4, 2016, https://mobile.twitter.com/realDonaldTrump/status/634765744673267712?ref_src=twsrc%5Etfw

91. Alinsky, S. *Rules for Radicals*. New York: Random House, 1971: 116–117.

92. Ibid., 129.

93. Schwartz, Ian. "Trump: There Will Be 'Riots' If I'm Leading in Delegates and Don't Win Nomination," *RealClear Politics*, March 16, 2016, accessed April 5, 2016, http://www.realclearpolitics.com/video/2016/03/16/trump_there_will_be_riots_if_im_leading_in_delegates_and_dont_win_nomination.html

94. Alinsky. *Rules for Radicals.* 134.

95. Hains, Tim. "Trump: Bill Clinton 'was impeached for lying!': CNN: 'What does that have to do with Hillary?'" *Real Clear Politics*, May 9, 2016, accessed April 7, 2016, http://www.realclearpolitics.com/video/2016/05/09/trump_bill_clinton_was_impeached_for_lying_cnn_what_does_that_have_to_do_with_hillary.html

96. Guest, Steve. "Trump: Hillary is 'one of the all time great enablers,'" *The Daily Caller*, April 29, 2016, accessed April 17, 2016, http://dailycaller.com/2016/04/29/trump-hillary-is-one-of-the-all-time-great-enablers/

97. The scandal is that she kept official e-mails on a personal server and kept classified e-mails on an unclassified server.

98. Byrnes, Jesse. "Trump: Clinton 'should suffer' for e-mails." *The Hill*, May 4, 2016, accessed April 12, 2016, http://thehill.com/blogs/ballot-box/presidential-races/278636-trump-clinton-should-suffer-for-emails

99. Miller, S.A. "Americans See a Dishonest Democrat They Dislike vs. an Old Socialist, Poll Shows," *The Washington Times*, February 23, 2016, accessed April 3, 2016, http://www.washingtontimes.com/news/2016/feb/23/americans-call-hillary-clinton-dishonest-bernie-sa/

100. Walker, Hunter. "Donald Trump Praises His Own 'Great' Debate Performance: 'I Am a Winner,'" *Business Insider*, August 6, 2015, accessed April 5, 2016, http://www.businessinsider.com/trump-praises-his-own-great-performance-2015-8

101. Schwartz, Ian. "Trump: 'We will have so much winning if I get elected that you may get bored with winning," *RealClear Politics*, September 9, 2015, accessed April 1, 2016, http://www.realclearpolitics.com/video/2015/09/09/trump_we_will_have_so_much_winning_if_i_get_elected_that_you_may_get_bored_with_winning.html

102. Foss, Sarah. "Supporters See Trump, Sanders as Winners," *The Daily Gazette*, April 11, 2016, accessed April 13, 2016, http://www.dailygazette.com/weblogs/foss/2016/apr/11/0411_foss/

103. Team Fix. "Donald Trump's Very Happy Victory Speech, Annotated," *The Washington Post*, February 9, 2016, accessed April 11, 2016, https://www.washingtonpost.com/news/the-fix/wp/2016/02/09/the-anatomy-of-a-donald-trump-victory-speech/

104. Lozada, Carlos. "How Donald Trump Plays the Press, in His Own Words," *The Washington Post*, June 17, 2015, accessed April 10, 2016, https://www.washingtonpost.com/news/book-party/wp/2015/06/17/how-donald-trump-plays-the-press-in-his-own-words/

105. Postrel, Virginia. "Trump Isn't Just Campaigning. He's Selling His Supporters a Glamorous Life," *The Washington Post*, March 18, 2016, accessed April 4, 2016, https://www.washingtonpost.com/opinions/trump-is-selling-a-dream-his-supporters-are-buying/2016/03/18/5307698e-eb8f-11e5-bc08-3e03a5b41910_story.html

106. Ibid.

107. Rees, "What 18 Former *Apprentice* Candidates Really Think of Donald Trump."

3   The Great Insulter

People, organizations, social groups, and even countries insult each other every day. Many believe that people offend each other out of frustration, because of bad manners, or simply as a result of the satisfaction they gain from hurting other people. Similarly, Donald Trump's insults are commonly perceived to be a reflection of his aggressiveness, incivility, and impoliteness. However, not all the insults he uses are equal or even similar.[1] Some insults target the positive image of others or deny them certain rights. Some insults create distance between Trump and other people or blame them for actions taken by Trump. Some insults emphasize Trump's power over others or present other people as illegitimate or untrustworthy.

These observations reinforce the notion that Trump uses different types of insults in specific situations. He does not just want to offend others, but rather, by using insults, he wants to achieve a particular goal. Trump employs social insults to prove that he is better than others, to justify his behavior by blaming others for provoking it, to distance himself from others, to strip people of some privileges, to present himself as more powerful, and to emphasize his higher validity and social weight in comparison with others.

Those who identify themselves with Trump receive the same social benefits derived from his insults as he does. Trump supporters "feed" on Trump's insults of his/their adversaries in order to achieve similar feelings of high self-esteem and power, to stress difference with people they dislike, to emphasize their privileged position in comparison with others, to get rid of uncomfortable feelings of shame or guilt for inappropriate actions, and to feel validated in their views and positions. Trump supporters love his use of insults. They simultaneously benefit from and feel more empowered by them. Let's explore how specifically they achieve these goals.

Identity Insult

People strive for positive self-identity. We need to feel good about ourselves. We have a need to believe that we have desirable features, that we are likable and positively viewed by others. All these feelings and knowledge contribute to our self-esteem, making us happier and self-assured. But how can we achieve this high self-esteem? We can acknowledge our achievements and successes, our good deeds, and positive intentions, but this is not generally enough; we need other sources of positive self-worth. We compare ourselves to other people or groups and attribute negative features to them. For example, we may view others as less educated, impolite, and irresponsible. This process, referred to as favorable comparison, helps us feel better about ourselves and increases our self-esteem.[2] Being better than somebody else provides us with a foundation of self-worth and a positive outlook of ourselves. People with a stronger individual identity usually tend to compare themselves with other people and see fewer similarities between them and others. People with salient social identity usually tend to use comparison with other groups and emphasize differences between their group members and members of other groups.[3] In both cases, this comparative assessment, which describes us as better than others, helps us to have a more positive outlook of ourselves. This process explains why most of us have prejudices and biases. These prejudices and biases do not develop from our need to discriminate but rather are a result of our need for positive self-esteem and comparison with others that present us in a better light.

Such *identity insults* can be an effective tool in increasing self-esteem through favorable comparison. People who use identity insults have a need to boost their own self-respect and confidence. Identity insults help the insulting side attribute negative features, dishonest motivations, and foul values to others, allowing them to portray their actions as destructive or flawed. Identity insults usually involve a comparison with the insulted party and a description of that party as having negative features or intentions. Thus identity insults employed by Trump serve a deep need of his supporters to increase or preserve their self-esteem.

Trump has used identity insults directly against his political opponents. Faced with tough competition from his Republican rival, Ted Cruz, in Texas, Trump used identity insult to strengthen a negative image of Cruz as a liar, which he had created earlier. He posted an image on Instagram superimposing Cruz's head on actor Jim Carrey's body from the film poster for the 1997 comedy *Liar Liar* (Martosko, 2015).[4] Although not original—a similar superimposed head of then president Bill Clinton was on the cover page of the *Weekly Standard* magazine when the movie was first released—the humor tends to be remembered and associated with the insulted. He also used Instagram to raise negative perceptions of Hilary Clinton as a liar: "Who should star in a reboot of Liar Liar—Hillary Clinton or Ted Cruz? Let me know."[5] Through this insult, Trump engaged his supporters in unfavorably comparing two of his major opponents. These identity insults not only succeeded in reducing any positive perceptions his supporters had regarding his two strongest opponents but also provided them with a feeling of high self-esteem in comparison with the voters who support these "liars." Trump supporters feel they were superior to others because they have been able to see through the other candidates and identify them for who they really are: liars.

Trump has also used identity insults in order to create a positive self-image among his supporters. Complaining that Megyn Kelly, the Fox New journalist, had treated him unfairly during the first Republican presidential debate, Trump accused her of being biased against him. He demanded she be removed from the second Fox News debate as a moderator and refused to participate in the debate when his request was denied. In response to her critical questions during the third debate, which succeeded in generating a less than favorable image of Trump, he launched a series of attacks against the news anchor and her image. In his identity insults, he called her "crazy," "average," "sick," and called upon his supporters to boycott her show because it was "always a hit on" him.[6] He also described Kelly as a bad journalist with low ratings. Trump even went as far as to say that Kelly was attacking him in order to increase her popularity. On the following Saturday morning, Trump said that Kelly's show was "terrible" and that her "ratings would totally tank" if she wasn't constantly covering him. He also tweeted, "Highly overrated & crazy @megynkelly is always complaining about Trump and yet she devotes her shows to me. Focus on others, Megyn!"[7] This identity insult aimed at stripping Kelly of her positive identity and image as a rising star journalist in turn increased the self-esteem of Trump supporters because they were backing the more popular leader.

Projection Insult

In the description of identity insult, I explored how positive identity is critical and illustrated the ways in which people use their own positive features and achievements, as well as favorable comparison with others, to increase their self-esteem. The question about what to do if you have done something wrong, done something that was negative, or was aggressive or unfair toward others still remains to be answered. How are people able to maintain their self-confidence and self-respect? One way to justify their behavior is by projecting negative intentions onto others. "We committed violent acts not because we were aggressive, but because they threatened us and we had to defend ourselves." "I deceived you not because I am dishonest, but because you were trying to mislead me and I needed to protect myself." Stressing that other peoples' behavior provokes one's own actions helps reduce one's responsibility and preserves one's perception of one's own positive self-image.

Similarly, if people face their own negative behavior, they experience conflicted feelings between the positive views they hold of themselves and a negative assessment of their actions. With this discomfort, referred to as cognitive dissonance,[8] people see a conflict between their expectations regarding how they should behave and their actual behavior. People are highly motivated to maintain consistency in their views. Generally, they prefer to maintain their positive self-image and consistent beliefs and thus usually change their view depending on the situation. "I was late not because I am not well organized, but because traffic was unpredictable." "We failed this project not because we did not have the required proficiencies, but because the existing information was inconsistent." In both situations—projection and cognitive dissonance—people justify their behavior by attributing negative intentions and features to other people or by blaming them for a given situation.[9]

This validation process of negative behavior can be supported by *projection insults*. Insulters use *projection insults* to justify particular actions or deny their own negative features by attributing them to others or to a situation created by others. It is routinely used when people face some consequences of their bad behavior and blame others for provoking it. Insulters are not happy about their actions and want to preserve their positive self-image. Consequently, they look for possible justifications for their behavior and usually blame the target of their negative actions, accusing them of provoking their conduct. They can also blame people close to them in order to justify their inability to be effective in other areas.

Trump has been actively using projection insults to defend his biased remarks. Responding to Trump's position about preventing Muslims from entering the U.S., Hilary Clinton stressed that his words are provoking more conflict. She said that Donald J. Trump "is becoming ISIS['s] best recruiter. They are going to people showing videos of Donald Trump insulting Islam and Muslims in order to recruit more radical jihadists."[10] Trump immediately responded with a projection insult, denying his responsibility and blaming Clinton for creating the conflict in the first place. Trump tweeted, "It's the Democrats' total weakness & incompetence that gave rise to ISIS—not a tape of Donald Trump that was an admitted Hillary lie!"[11] To increase the impact of this projection insult, on NBC's *Today* show Trump said, "She should apologize. She lies about emails, she lies about Whitewater, she lies about everything. She will be a disaster about everything as president of the United States."[12] This projection insult was grounded in already existing concerns among likely voters about Mrs. Clinton's honesty. It helped Trump's supporters to justify their own biases and prejudices—they understood their positions as the result of the mistaken policies and general missteps of the current administration.

Trump has consistently used projection insults to justify why many mass media outlets present him in a negative light. In his interview with CBS News anchor Scott Pelley, Trump stated,

> You know, some of the media is among the worst people I've ever met. I mean a pretty good percentage is really a terrible group of people. They

write lies, they write false stories. They know they're false. It makes no difference. And frankly, I don't call it thin-skinned, I'm angry.[13]

He explained this negative coverage as the desperate need of mass media to use his popularity to increase their ratings. "I'm on a lot of covers," Trump said in the *60 Minutes* interview. "I think maybe more than almost any supermodel. I think more than any supermodel. But in a way that is a sign of respect, people are respecting what you are doing."[14] For example, he accused *Politico* of covering him inaccurately, calling *Politico* journalists "clowns" who are "totally dishonest."[15] In his projection insult, he suggested that *Politico* was "losing lots of money" and desperately needed to use his popularity. This projection insult, thus, provided his supporters with a clear explanation of why mass media coverage of Trump was and continues to be negative. It also reassured them that in reality, it was a "sign of respect" and Trump is the most popular person in the U.S.

Divergence Insult

In our lives, we interact with many people, trying to stay close to some of them and distancing ourselves from others. We create distance between ourselves and others by stressing similarities with people we like and differences with people we don't. The more similar we are and the more we share with other people, the closer we become to them. The more differences we have with people, the more we tend to emphasize these distinctions and reduce similarities in order to increase the distance between ourselves and other people. In the former case, we are seen as one group with similar interests, values, and aspirations. In the latter case, we are seen as completely separate, with different views and understandings of the world. This social boundary involves meanings of difference and similarity between people and is therefore defined by the relationship between "them" and "us."[16] Building and changing our relationships always involves changes to social boundaries by making them either more permeable or impervious. To define whether a social boundary will be more or less inclusive, people focus on the resemblances and disparities between themselves and others.[17]

Changes to social boundaries in relationships sometimes can be perceived as threatening. Conversely, members of high-status groups strengthen their identification with their group and protect the group's existing boundaries.[18] High-status groups will often create policies and take actions that close boundaries and prevent associations with groups of lower status.[19] People and groups recognize clear boundaries that represent distinctive ways of life and can actively resist when they perceive these boundaries to be endangered or threatened.[20] People use every possible means to increase their distance from these other persons and groups. Thus people usually create social boundaries to help defend their own group from the perceived threat of outsiders, and in doing so, further define reasons for exclusion.[21]

Divergence insults can help enhance differences and social boundaries between different sides and highlight the distance between them. Insulting people usually stresses distinctions between them and those they insult by emphasizing different ways of life, customs, traditions, values, beliefs, perceptions, and attitudes. Divergence insults can emphasize differences in appearance, gender, age, place of residence, ethnicity, race, political affiliation, and religion.

Building on negative widespread perceptions concerning violent crime rates in Mexico and beliefs that Mexico is exploiting the U.S., Trump has created a divergence insult that supports these positions. Reacting to the dramatic prison break by Mexico's most powerful drug lord, Joaquin "El Chapo" Guzman, Trump quickly focused on the disparities between the U.S. and Mexico: "Likewise, billions of dollars gets brought into Mexico through the border. We get the killers, drugs & crime, they get the money!" Trump's subsequent tweet helped him to justify his stance on building a wall along the U.S./Mexican border: "El Chapo and the Mexican drug cartels use the border unimpeded like it was a vacuum cleaner, sucking drugs and death right into the U.S."[22] Thus Trump has focused on emphasizing the importance of both social and physical boundaries. These divergent insults have empowered his supporters who already had negative perceptions toward Mexico and its people. They believe that Trump can protect them from the criminality and danger of Mexico.

Utilizing the fear of radical Islam in the U.S., Trump has also created a divergence insult in order to increase distance between Muslims and the U.S. He framed Islam as a religion of hate: "I think Islam hates us. There's something there—there's a tremendous hatred there. There's a tremendous hatred. We have to get to the bottom of it. There is an unbelievable hatred of us."[23] This insult supports existing fears among his followers and justifies their fear of Islam's spread and prejudice against Muslims. They feel inspired by his ideas to put a "temporary" ban on Muslims entering the country and to "certainly implement" a database system tracking Muslims in the U.S. These ideas make Trump's supporters feel more secure and justified in their intolerance.

Relative Insult

It's no secret that people tend to compare their social positions, available resources, and possibilities with what they had in the past and what they expect to have in the future. If people believe that their life situation has worsened or their expectations are not being fulfilled, they have a tendency to feel depressed. This feeling is called relative deprivation. [24] In the former case, if people think that their social position has become less stable or lower within given power relations, that they have lost certain resources, and the likelihood of a positive change has decreased, they experience temporal deprivation.[25] The perception of deprivation or of being disadvantaged more often than not comes from comparisons with others rather than comparing people in past situations or expected future situations. It is important to note that these negative changes or reduced possibilities can simply be imagined by individuals or groups rather than being a result of objective assessment or based in reality.

To reduce this feeling of deprivation and deficiency, people tend to think of themselves as superior to others by using *relative* insults. It is most frequently used when people are trying to restore a perceived imbalance concerning resources or social positions, or when seeking to challenge a situation that is believed to be unjust. People deny certain rights of others and emphasize their own privileged position through inclusive rights to control, to make decisions, and to perform actions and define the connotations of events and situations. It is important to understand that insulters, whether they realize it or not, feel deprived in comparison to their previous position, expectations, and, most importantly, in comparison to other groups. They believe that they deserve more and should have more rights—or at least as many rights—as others, but are not treated well or are discriminated against in comparison with other people or groups. They are looking for things to be restored to how they once were and desperately want to stress the lower status, resources, or abilities of another party. In all these cases, a feeling of relative deprivation provokes people to resort to insulting behavior in order to improve their position in comparison to others.

As a finalist, Trump expected to be nominated *Time* magazine's "Person of the Year" (for 2015). He was disappointed when the magazine selected Angela Merkel, the German chancellor, instead. He refused to accept that his candidacy was controversial and blamed the selection committee for making the wrong choice. "I told you @TIME Magazine would never pick me as person of the year despite being the big favorite. They picked the person who is ruining Germany." [26] He stated that Merkel should "be ashamed of herself" for allowing a massive group of Syrian refugees to enter Germany. This relative insult helped Trump and his supporters cope with the loss of the expected title. Instead of feeling disappointment, his supporters felt anger toward the magazine and its nomination of a supposedly undeserving foreign leader. By comparing himself to Merkel, who "is ruining" Germany with her immigration policies, Trump presented himself as a leader who would protect the nation from similar misguided policies. He used the dissatisfaction of his supporters to further promote his popularity among them and to show that he has more rights to be the most popular leader.

Trump also repudiated the protests of Black activists, stressing that they are trying to take advantage of other racial groups. He denies structural problems, racial biases, and discrimination, implying that the Black Lives Matters movement does not have the right to challenge the established social order and does not belong in the U.S. When asked what he would do about the protests against racially motivated violence that took place in South Carolina, Trump stated,

> There's no such thing as racism anymore. We've had a black president so it's not a question anymore. Are they saying black lives should matter more than White lives or Asian lives? If Black lives matter, then go back to Africa. We'll see how much they matter there.[27]

In this relative insult, Trump not only rejects the importance of the Black Lives Matters movement but also rejects the rights of Black activists to represent the broader U.S. This insult strongly resonates with those supporters who resent the existence of a protected class of citizens and those who have racial prejudice, believing that the movement poses a threat to Whites' position in America.

Power Insult

Power relations underlie every form of communication among people, thus shaping the ways in which we see others and ourselves. Established power balances dictate the ways in which people behave around other people. To that effect, one person engaged in an interaction with others may have more power or equal power to the person or persons they are interacting with. People follow the orders of their supervisors, give instructions to people they supervise, and provide opinions and advice to fellow co-workers. For example, a master's student may take directions from a professor, give advice to undergraduate students, and discuss his work with other master's students. Power relations also can be asymmetric when people have power in different spheres. For example, a buyer has the power to withdraw from a purchase if she does not like the product, and the seller has the power to revoke a sale if the buyer's offer is too low.

People in power can have authority over others by virtue of the resources under their control. First, people in power can bestow welfare values: they can influence the conditions of other people, including their well-being, wealth, skills, and knowledge. For example, they can control salary rates or other compensation, access to medical services, and education. Second, people in power can influence the perceptions of others, including the respect they receive from others and the reputation they have in a community. They usually employ a system of reward and punishment to solidify their dominance. Thus they can provide or remove welfare values—for example, bonus pay—or increase or decrease the degree to which members of a community regard another person in a positive light. Perceiving power as a zero-sum game, people tend to fight for and over the sources of such power and how to influence power dynamics.

Insults can enable people to redefine existing balances of power. *Power insults* occur in situations of competition for coercive power, which can be real or perceived by people. This insult helps to decrease the absolute or relative power of others in comparison with an insulter, thus providing the insulter with more influence and authority. People who feel less powerful in their relationships and have fewer abilities to change the situation or alter the other side's behavior typically employ *power insults*. They do so because they have a desire for more access to coercive power or a need to restore a previous balance of power in order to control or lead other people or groups. Thus they use power insults to challenge the power of others or to strip the other side of authority.

Trump has frequently employed power insults to enhance or restore his perceived supremacy and control. He has employed power insults in competition with political rivals. Faced with stiff competition from Jeb Bush in the New Hampshire primary, Trump used several power insults to diminish the influence of his opponent. Bush invited his mother, Barbara Bush, to support him in the campaign. Asking to comment on Trump in her interview to CNN, she said, "I'm sick of him."[28] Trump immediately responded with the tweet, "Wow, Jeb Bush, whose campaign is a total disaster, had to bring in mommy to take a slap at me. Not nice!"[29] In this power insult, Trump not only highlighted the ineffectiveness of Bush's campaign but also portrayed him as a powerless individual who requires the support of his mother. To his supporters, this insult positioned Trump as a powerful man, whereas Bush was portrayed as a weak and incapable "momma's boy." This power insult empowered Trump supporters, providing them with feelings of superiority.

In his competition with Ted Cruz, Trump also utilized power insults. When former presidential nominee Mitt Romney supported Ted Cruz in his home state of Utah, Trump immediately responded with an insult. Romney posted on his Facebook that he was going to vote for Cruz during the Republican caucuses in Utah: "I will vote for Senator Cruz and I encourage others to do so as well, so that we can have an open convention and nominate a Republican."[30] Trump responded with a power insult, diminishing the influence of Cruz: "Going to Salt Lake City, Utah, for a big rally. Lyin' Ted Cruz should not be allowed to win there—Mormons don't like LIARS! I beat Hillary."[31] Knowing that the majority of Utah residents are Mormons and share this faith with Mitt Romney, Trump also attempted to diminish the influence of Romney there and tweeted twice: "Failed presidential candidate Mitt Romney, the man who 'choked' and let us all down, is now endorsing Lyin' Ted Cruz. This is good for me!" and "Failed Presidential Candidate Mitt Romney was campaigning with John Kasich & Marco Rubio, and now he is endorsing Ted Cruz. Mitt Romney is a mixed up man who doesn't have a clue. No wonder he lost!"[32] Thus in this power insult, Trump not only tried to reduce the power of Romney but also connected Cruz to Romney as a loser. It provided his followers with assurances that they were indeed supporting the winning candidate.

Legitimacy Insult

In comparison with coercion, legitimacy is based on respect for others and acceptance that particular people in positions of power have a right to influence the opinions and behaviors of other people.[33] Other people are expected to regard and accept this influence. How can people acquire legitimacy? Throughout our lives, we learn the norms and values that are embedded in our everyday interactions with others. We learn what is good behavior and what is bad; we realize which values are better and which are unacceptable. Through this process, we accept social norms and values as essential to our lives. Thus people who develop and protect them are perceived as legitimate and respected.[34]

In addition, legitimacy is connected with a shared social identity.[35] People interpret and evaluate power through the lens of their salient group membership; members of one group are considered as more representative of group goals and as more normative and persuasive. Thus political leaders become influential by employing the basic norms and ideas of social identity and increasing the overall perception of them as prototypical. To preserve legitimate power, its agents need to employ a constant process whereby they seek to legitimize themselves and delegitimize others.

Legitimacy insults initiate and promote a process that legitimizes insulters and delegitimizes the other side. Thus *legitimacy insults* help a person or a group to diminish the legality and rightfulness of the other side and to increase his own or his group's validity. Sometimes, both sides of a conflict can use the same attributes to portray others as illicit and illegitimate. Insulting people are usually not satisfied about their power positions and want to have more legitimacy and acceptance than the other side. They believe that they do their best to represent and support the fundamental values, norms, and attitudes associated with their group, and they want to be perceived as prototypical and legitimate leaders. They also want to be appreciated for their devotion and see respect of other people as an obstacle to this gratitude. Thus they see themselves in competition for legitimate power and leadership.

Trump has used legitimacy insults to delegitimize his political rival, Hillary Clinton. Responding to allegations of sexism and the maltreatment of women, Trump sought to emphasize the womanizing behavior of her husband in the past. He referred to the record of marital infidelity and alleged sexual misconducts of Bill Clinton. "Hillary Clinton has announced that she is letting her husband out to campaign but HE'S DEMONSTRATED A PENCHANT FOR SEXISM, so inappropriate!"[36] Trump also employed his female staff, spokeswoman Katrina Pierson, to strengthen this legitimacy insult toward the Clintons. She called Hillary Clinton a hypocrite for criticizing Trump as sexist while she remains the wife of Bill Clinton who had multiple extramarital affairs and had to settle sexual harassment lawsuits and admitted sexual relationships with several employees. "Hillary Clinton has some nerve to talk about the war on women and the bigotry toward women when she has a serious problem in her husband," Pierson told CNN's Kate Bolduan.[37] In order to further delegitimize the Clintons, Trump accused Hilary Clinton of being cruel to other women: "I can think of quite a few women who have been bullied by Hillary Clinton to hide her husband's misogynist, sexist secrets."[38] The use of this legitimacy insult aimed to decrease the validity of any accusation made by Clinton concerning the womanizing or sexist behavior of Trump. This insult represented the Clintons as illegitimate in their criticisms of Trump's behavior in his relations with women, thus increasing Trump's validity among his would-be supporters.

Trump has also employed legitimacy insults to question the rightfulness of his critics. Senator John McCain was a navy pilot during the Vietnam War and spent over five years in prison, locked in solitary confinement, and he was repeatedly tortured. McCain accused Trump of "firing up the crazies" with his controversial statements. Trump, who escaped serving in Vietnam through four student deferments, created an insult to decrease the legitimacy of McCain. During a gathering in Iowa, Trump stated, "In addition to doing a lousy job of taking care of our Vets, John McCain let us down by losing to Barack Obama in his run for President!"[39] In this insult, Trump presented McCain as both incapable of winning the White House for the Republican Party and addressing the needs of his fellow veterans. Trump also added, "He was a war hero because he was captured. I like people who weren't captured."[40] In this legitimacy insult, he diminished the position of McCain as a hero, and thus showed his supporters that McCain's claims were illegitimate. This insult empowered them by contributing to their view of Trump as a winner who would not be captured and would win the election.

Being a Bully

In high school, insults help students to increase their status in relation to their peers, stressing their privileged position. Students from a high-status group describe their side as a "side where the good people sit."[41] Children from high-status social groups receive the most attention from others in comparison to other students and are considered "cool," "popular," and "mean."[42] The position of popularity is attractive to many students, and some of them seek to be associated with the members of high-status groups. However, popular students protect their position and only allow people who are privileged or who have the potential to be popular to join them. Their peers describe students with perceived high levels of popularity as dominant and aggressive.[43] Being nice is perceived as a threat to the established status because polite behavior creates equality. Moreover, to maintain their high social status over many years, students need to become more aggressive, particularly through the use of insults toward their outgroup peers.[44] This form of aggression usually involves different types of relative insults, such as intentionally excluding a peer from social plans for a party, movie night, or just going out as a group, as well as spreading gossip about a peer or hurting a peer through the use of harsh words.[45]

Trump employs the behavior of a "popular" person who can bully and insult people of lower social status groups. His supporters see themselves as a part of his clique, thus acquiring a feeling of superiority and a higher position in the social hierarchy. The ability to be mean to others and the "power to insult" others are what connect Trump supporters within his hierarchy. They believe that as people with a higher status, they can be mean to other people and insult them, thereby cementing their privileged position. Thus Trump supporters see his bullying behavior and meanness as a sign of his popularity and feel empowered by his bullying and harassment.

This short overview of the insults and bullying behavior of Trump shows us that Trump instrumentally uses them to empower his supporters. Through connection to his insults, his supporters acquire a higher sense of self-esteem and positive social identity, which in turn justifies their prejudice and discriminative behaviors and allows them to distance themselves from people they detest and strip them of particular rights. They also feel more powerful than supporters of opposing candidates and more validated in their views and positions. Through Trump's insults and harassments of others, his supporters are acquiring a perception of higher social status and a feeling of being superior within the established social hierarchy. In the next chapter, I will discuss how Trump enables his supporters to regain a sense of superiority that they feel has been slipping away as well as their feeling of being threatened by other groups group in society.

Notes

1. Korostelina, K. V. *Political Insults: How Offenses Escalate Conflict*. Oxford, USA: Oxford University Press, 2014.
2. Tajfel H, and J. C. Turner. "The Social Identity Theory of Intergroup Behaviour," in *Psychology of Intergroup Relations* S. Worchel, and W. G. Austin 2nd ed., Chicago: Nelson-Hall, 1985.
3. Turner, J. C., Hogg, M. A., Oakes, P. J., Reicher, S. D., and Wetherell, M. S., *Rediscovering the Social Group: A Self-Categorization Theory*, Cambridge, MA, US: Basil Blackwel, (1987), 50.
4. Martosko, D. "Fresh from Primary Victories, Trump Is Back Doing What He Does Best—Trolling Ted Cruz as 'Liar Liar' with New Social Media Poll," *Daily Mail*, March 17, 2016, accessed April 17, 2016, http://www.dailymail.co.uk/news/article-3497864/Fresh-primary-victories-Trump-doing-does-best-trolling-Ted-Cruz-Liar-Liar-new-social-media-poll.html
5. Trump, D. "Liar Liar," *Instagram*. Retrieved from: https://www.instagram.com/p/BDEHPEgmhRv/
6. Garcia, A. "Read Donald Trump's Tweets about Megyn Kelly and Fox's Response," *CNN Money*, March 19, 2016, accessed April 15, 2016 http://money.cnn.com/2016/03/19/media/donald-trump-megyn-kelly-tweets-fox/
7. Ibid.
8. Festinger, L. *A Theory of Cognitive Dissonance*. Stanford, CA: Stanford University Press, 1957.
9. Ross, L. "The Intuitive Psychologist and His Shortcomings: Distortions in the Attribution Process," in *Advances in Experimental Social Psychology*, ed. L. Berkowitz, New York: Academic Press. 10 (1977): 173–220, Jones, E. E. and Harris, V. A. "The attribution of attitudes." *Journal of Experimental Social Psychology* 3, no 1(1967): 1–24.
10. Rappeport, A. "Donald Trump Wants Apology from Hillary Clinton Over 'Lies'," *NY Times*, December 21, 2015, accessed April 20, 2016, http://www.nytimes.com/politics/first-draft/2015/12/21/donald-trump-wants-apology-from-hillary-clinton-over-lies/?_r=0
11. Ibid.
12. Ibid.
13. Calderone, M., and Robinson, J. "43 Times Donald Trump Has Attacked the Media as a Presidential Candidate," *Huffington Post*, September 18, 2015, accessed April 19, 2016 http://www.huffingtonpost.com/entry/donald-trump-has-attacked-the-media-many-many-times_us_56059e0de4b0af3706dc3cce.
14. Ibid.
15. Mullen, B. "Donald Trump Launches Two-Tweet Tirade against *Politico*," *Poynter*, October 7, 2015, accessed April 25, 2016 http://www.poynter.org/2015/donald-trump-launches-two-tweet-tirade-against-politico/377412/
16. Barth, F. *Process and Form in Social Life*. London: Routledge and Kegan Paul, 1981.
17. Horowitz, D. L. "Ethnic Identity." in *Ethnicity, Theory and Experience*, eds. Glazer, N. and Moynihan, D. Cambridge: Harvard University Press, 1975 p.111–40.
18. Ellemers, N., Spears, R., and Doosje, B. ""Sticking together or falling apart: Ingroup identification as a psychological determinant of group commitment versus individual mobility." *Journal of Personality and Social Psychology* 72(1997): 617–626.

19. Hutnik N. *Ethnic Minority Identity.* Oxford: Clarendon Press, 1991.
20. Cohen, A. P. *The Symbolic Construction of Community.* London: Tavistock, 1985; Cohen, A. P., "Belonging: The experience of culture," in *Symbolising Boundaries: Identity and Diversity in British Cultures,* ed. A. P. Cohen, Manchester: Manchester University Press. (1986): 1–17.
21. Tilly, C. *Identities, Boundaries and Social Ties.* Boulder: Paradigm, 2005.
22. FoxNews. "Trump on 'El Chapo' Prison Break: 'I Told You So!,'" *Fox News Insider,* July 13, 2015, accessed April 17, 2016, http://insider.foxnews.com/2015/07/13/trump-drug-lord-el-chapos-prison-break-mexico-i-told-you-so
23. Schleifer, Theodore. "Donald Trump: 'I Think Islam Hates Us,'" *CNN,* March 10, 2016, accessed April 19, 2016, http://www.cnn.com/2016/03/09/politics/donald-trump-islam-hates-us/
24. Davis, J. A. "A formal interpretation of the theory of relative deprivation." in *Sociometry* 22, (1959): 280–296; Gurr, T. R. *Minorities at Risk: A Global View of Ethnopolitical Conflict.* Washington, DC: United States Institute of Peace, 1993; Runciman, W. G., *Relative Deprivation and Social Justice: A Study of Attitudes to Social Inequality in Twentieth Century England.* Berkeley: University of California Press, 1966.
25. Albert, S. "Temporal comparison theory," in *Psychological Review* 84, (1977): 485–503.
26. Scott, E., and Kopan, T. "Trump: TIME's Person of the Year 'Ruining Germany'," *CNN,* December 9, 2015, accessed April 22, 2016, http://www.cnn.com/2015/12/09/politics/donald-trump-time-magazine-person-of-the-year/
27. "Donald Trump 'If Black Lives Don't Matter, Then Go Back to Africa," *Celebtricity,* accessed April 17, 2016, http://www.celebtricity.com/donald-trump-if-black-lives-dont-matter-then-go-back-to-africa/
28. Gangel, Jamie. ""Interview with Barbara Bush and Jeb Bush,"" *CNN,* accessed April 18, 2016, http://www.cnn.com/videos/us/2016/02/05/barbara-bush-sick-of-trump-gangel-intv-lead.cnn
29. Allen, Cooper. "Trump: Jeb Bush 'had to bring in mommy to take a slap at me,'" *USA TODAY,* February 6, 2016, accessed April 18, 2016, http://www.usatoday.com/story/news/politics/onpolitics/2016/02/06/jeb-bush-donald-trump/79922352/
30. McCaskill, Nolan D. "Mitt Romney Says He's Voting for Ted Cruz," *Politico,* March 18, 2016, accessed April 20, 2016, http://www.politico.com/blogs/2016-gop-primary-live-updates-and-results/2016/03/mitt-romney-vote-ted-cruz-utah-220974
31. Ibid.
32. Ibid.
33. Herbert Kelman. "Reflections on the Social and Psychological Processes of Legitimization and Delegitimization," in *The Psychology of Legitimacy: Emergin Perspectives on Ideology, Justice, and Intergroup Relations,* ed. J. T. Jost, and B. Major, Cambridge: Cambridge University Press. (2001): 54–73.
34. Ibid.,67.
35. Wenzel, Michael, and Prita Jobling. "Legitimacy of regulatory authorities as a function of inclusive identification and power over ingroups and outgroups." *European Journal of Social Psychology* 36, no. 2 (2006): 239–258, doi:10.1002/ejsp.298.
36. de Vries, K. "Trump Slams Bill Clinton's 'Sexism' in Attack on Hillary Clinton," *CNN,* December 27, 2015, accessed April 122, 2016, http://www.cnn.com/2015/12/26/politics/donald-trump-bill-clinton-sexism/

37. Ibid.
38. Ibid.
39. Alexander, H. "Donald Trump Tells John McCain: 'I Like People Who Weren't Captured'," *The Telegraph*, July 18, 2015. April 21, 2016, http://www.telegraph.co.uk/news/worldnews/republicans/11748859/Donald-Trump-tells-John-McCain-I-like-people-who-werent-captured.html
40. Ibid.
41. Ibid.
42. Merten, D. E. ""The meaning of meanness: Popularity, competition, and conflict among junior high school girls."" *Sociology of Education* 70, (1997): 175–191.
43. Kwon, K., Lease, A. M., and Hoffman, L. ""The impact of clique membership on children's social behavior and status nominations."" *Social Development* 21, no 1(2012): 150–169.
44. Pokhrel, P., Sussman, S., Black, D., and Sun, P. "Peer group self-identification as a predictor of relational and physical aggression among high school students." *Journal of School Health*, 80, no.5 (2010): 249–258.
45. Ibid.

4   Angry as Hell

To gain voter support, politicians tend to show they are both sympathetic to the problems people are facing and empathetic to their feelings. In comparison with other candidates who show understanding of the American public's needs and empathize with them, Trump displays emotions similar to the American people instead. He shows his supporters how to amplify their emotions, and they eagerly learn from him. He is just as angry and frustrated as they are, and he is just as furious and energetic as they want to be. This display of mirrored emotions connects his supporters deeply to one another and also to their leader, Trump, providing a strong, overall sense of unity. Trump's emotional appeal is, therefore, based on the frustration of his supporters, their feelings of deprivation and threat, and, interestingly, his self-adulation and narcissistic behavior.

Addressing Frustration

When people realize they are unable to achieve their goals, change their existing troubled situation, or improve their lives, they experience heightened levels of psychological tension, which impacts many of their emotions. They feel dissatisfied, depressed, and unhappy. This frustration, especially if it exists for extended periods, produces deep feelings of anger that can be connected to either the actual source of the frustration or to other people. People need to reduce this tension and often become aggressive toward others who they blame as the source of their frustration. On the other hand, displaced aggression is directed toward people whose fault is only that they are accessible or vulnerable.[1]

Trump employs several types of aggression. The first of which is retaliatory aggression.[2] When people feel somebody is behaving aggressively toward them or has offended them, they typically respond with retaliation. Although provocation can be real or imagined, people tend to behave aggressively toward the offender. By responding with hostility, people not only reduce their frustration but also create an impression of being strong and powerful. They believe people who do not retaliate are weak. Moreover, if people believe the offenders are attacking their character, they typically retaliate in any way they can.[3]

Throughout his campaign, Trump has swiftly responded to every accusation or insult from his opponents. In the *Art of the Deal*, Trump writes,

> When people wrong you, go after those people because it is a good feeling and because other people will see you doing it. I love getting even . . . I go after people, and you know what? People do not play around with me as much as they do with others. They know that if they do, they are in for a big fight.[4]

Trump's reactions are often exaggerated and much more offensive than the initial attack. When Rafael Cruz, the father of Ted Cruz, stated that "the alternative" to his son "could be the destruction of America," Trump immediately responded: "I think it's a disgrace that he's allowed to do it, I think it's a disgrace that he's allowed to say it."[5] Trump went on to explain this position by claiming that Cruz's father may have played some role in the assassination of John F. Kennedy. Trump referred to a *National Enquirer* story about Rafael Cruz appearing in a photo with the assassin shortly before the murder: "I mean what was he doing—what was he doing with Lee Harvey Oswald shortly before the death, before the shooting? It's horrible."[6] Cruz immediately denied the accusation: "Now let's be clear: This is nuts. This is not a reasonable position. This is just kooky."[7] Trump instantly reacted, describing Cruz as a desperate candidate who could not handle pressure and was likely to break in reaction to stress. "Today's ridiculous outburst only proves what I have been saying for a long time, that Ted Cruz does not have the temperament to be President of the United States."[8] In the following tweet, Trump went further, comparing Cruz to his toddler: "That was an impressive meltdown . . . Desperate but impressive. Reminded me of my 3 year old coming off a sugar high."[9] Trump supporters reacted to this feud, responding with more aggression and insults: "Cruz doesn't have a clue. Everything he does to try to bring in voters does the opposite affect." "Lyin' Ted's blood pressure is probably going through the roof." "Desperate and once again living up to why he's so hated."[10]

These tactics leave Trump's opponents open and unprepared to respond. The weakness of Trump's opponent's responses provide further evidence for his supporters that he is more powerful than his opponents. It empowers his followers to strike against those individuals and groups who disagree or protest.[11] When a protester tried to interrupt his speech at one of his rallies, Trump reacted immediately, stating, "Get 'em the hell out of here." The reaction of the crowd was particularly violent. Trump fans labeled the man a monkey. They punched and kicked the protester, pushing him to the ground, and stepping on his hands.[12] Trump sought to justify the violent reaction of his supporters, stressing they needed to be even more forceful in response to the aggression of protesters. At a press conference, he defended his supporters: "And I thought it was very, very appropriate. He was swinging. He was hitting people. And the audience hit back. And that's what we need a little bit more of."[13] Trump also encouraged the retaliatory aggression of his supporters. At a rally in Iowa, he said,

> There may be somebody with tomatoes in the audience. If you see somebody getting ready to throw a tomato, knock the crap out of them, would you? Seriously. Okay? Just knock the hell—I promise you, I will pay for the legal fees.[14]

This justification and encouragement of retaliatory aggression has electrified some of Trump's supporters, vindicating actions that would have previously been frowned upon.

When Julia Ioffe wrote an article about Melania Trump, Trump's current wife, for *GQ*, Mrs. Trump responded with criticism: "There are numerous inaccuracies in this article including certain statements about my family and claims on personal matters."[15] Within one day of the article's publication, Ioffe started receiving threats and offensive messages from Trump supporters. They referred to her Jewish heritage, telling her she should be sent to a concentration camp, burned in an oven, or shot in the head. She received calls inquiring about overnight casket delivery and recordings of Hitler's speeches.[16] Trump said he did "not condone violence in any shape,"[17] but he would not discourage his supporters from engaging in the retaliatory aggression suffered by the likes of Ioffe and other journalists. Instead of condemning the hateful actions among this group of his followers, Trump responded: "I don't have a message to the fans. A woman wrote an article that's inaccurate."[18]

Trump has also employed retaliatory aggression against the current administration. Trump voters are dissatisfied with the policies of the current administration of President Obama. Building on frustration connected with increased unemployment and the decreasing social and financial status of White blue-collar workers, Trump has shown he is not only in touch with the anger and frustration of his followers but also feels it:

> People come [to Trump campaign events] with tremendous passion and love for their country. . ... When they see what's going on in this country, they have anger that's unbelievable. They have anger. They love this

country. They don't like seeing bad trade deals. They don't like seeing higher taxes. They don't like seeing a loss of their jobs. . .. And I see it.[19]

In order to resonate with his supporters' feelings of frustration and anger, Trump has aggressively and directly attacked President Obama, referring to him as the worst president in America's history.[20] Trump added, "He has just been a disaster for our country. . . He has done such a lousy job as president."[21] Trump supporters share this aggression toward President Obama, questioning his political motives, policies, religious sympathies, and birthplace. They praise Trump for publicly questioning whether Obama was in fact born in Hawaii and whether he was eligible to be president of the U.S. As one supporter stated, "In our Constitution, it says that the president has to be an American citizen. I'm still wondering where is he really from. What is this man's background?"[22] Another supporter echoed this sentiment, calling President Obama "too much of a Muslim" and an "Islamist sympathizer." In general, more than 60 percent of Trump supporters believe that President Obama is a Muslim masquerading as a Christian in order to be elected.[23] As one supporter said, "We live under the rule of a Muslim dictator. But not for much longer, thankfully." Another supporter agreed: "Obama HATES America and is punishing Americans."[24]

To address his supporters' dissatisfaction with the Obama administration, Trump has also frequently used displaced aggression.[25] People can feel frustration toward someone because they think that person is either holding them back or because they feel someone is diminishing their ability to satisfy their rights or needs. For example, people are often unable to confront this person directly to change their situation through retaliation or by complaining because the offender occupies a stronger position or higher social status. Instead, they turn their displaced aggression toward innocent targets they perceive to be more vulnerable or weaker. The targets of such displaced aggression include persons or groups who occupy a lower social status and are less powerful, which typically means they are unable to retaliate. For example, a man can be criticized heavily by his supervisor but is unable to respond because he is afraid of losing his job. On the way home from work, he can take out his frustration on a fellow driver or even severely punish his children for minor infractions.

Trump helps his supporters to channel the frustration they have for Obama's immigration policies toward illegal immigrants. Their dissatisfaction is driven by cultural anxiety (perception of negative cultural change and cultural decline) as well as feelings of economic deprivation. Sixty-seven percent of Republicans say the American way of life and culture more broadly has gotten worse since the 1950s because of immigrants. More than 63 percent of White working-class Americans say they feel bothered when they come into contact with immigrants who do not speak English. Similarly, 66 percent of Republicans believe that immigrants are a burden on the country.[26] Many of Trump's followers believe many immigrants avoid paying taxes but widely receive benefits such as free public education, welfare, food stamps, and Medicaid. For example, one Trump supporter noted that so-called new Americans are flooding the country:

> The people that are coming in here from China, Indonesia and all of them countries, they're getting pregnant and coming here and having babies. They get everything and the people that were born here can't get everything.[27]

Another supporter echoed this sentiment, stating,

> I come home and someone's occupying my house and they're eating my food and then they're taking the kids from my bed; they're taking the money out of my pocket. Why should we have to support someone else and then make our kids suffer, our families suffer?[28]

Similarly to Republican voters, Trump supporters, which also include Democrats and independents, generally consider immigration a burden on the country and, as a result, support Trump's hardline policies toward immigration. Eighty-four percent of them favor building a wall along the U.S.-Mexico border.[29]

Trump has promised to enforce strict immigration laws, establish a nationwide e-verification system to "protect jobs for unemployed Americans," stop tuition benefits for illegal immigrants, and "cut-off federal grants to any city refusing to cooperate with federal law enforcement"[30] such as sanctuary cities. As frustration causes stress and discontent, aggression emerges as an inevitable part of behavior and strongly connects Trump to his supporters. They see his proposals as reflecting their concept of citizenship, which is premised on the exclusion of noncitizens from entitlements.

Together with aggression resulting from frustration, Trump has also actively used instrumental aggression. Such aggression does not result from anger or a need to retaliate. Instead, instrumental aggression is cold-blooded. It is employed as a way to achieve specific goals, obtain a desirable position, or to intimidate and invalidate others.[31] Throughout their lives, people learn this type of aggression can result in an easy win and desired rewards. As such, people create offenses against others in order to obtain more power and resources.

Trump has shown his supporters how to address a number of issues and, in turn, be rewarded and gain power through the use of aggression. Attacking his primary rival, Senator Cruz, Trump stated that Cruz could not run for president because he was born in Canada. Similarly to his doubts about President Obama, Trump confronted Cruz, denying his right to be president: "He was born in Canada. If you know and when we all studied our history lessons, you are supposed to be born in this country, so I just don't know how the courts will rule on this."[32] Following his statement, five Trump supporters filed a lawsuit challenging the eligibility of Senator Cruz to run for president. The lawsuit sought a judgment "declaring that Rafael Edward Cruz is ineligible to qualify/run/seek and be elected to the Office of the President of the United States of America" due to his Canadian birth.[33] The aim of this aggressive tactic was to question the legitimacy of Cruz as a presidential candidate and create doubt among his would-be supporters.

Similarly, Trump launched an attack on another rival, Jeb Bush. He connected Jeb to his brother, former president George W. Bush, accusing him of deceit regarding the Iraq War and dangerous policies.

They lied. They said there were weapons of mass destruction. There were none. And they knew there were none. There were no weapons of mass destruction . . . We spent $2 trillion, thousands of lives. . .. We should have never been in Iraq. We have destabilized the Middle East."[34]

He also blamed former president George W. Bush for not keeping America safe: "The World Trade Center came down during the reign of George Bush. He kept us safe? That is not safe."[35] Through these instrumental attacks, Trump aimed to diminish the influence of the Bush family, especially in states where they are well liked. This proved to be an effective strategy for Trump.

The Trump supporters saw these attacks as a demonstration of his strength. As one supporter said, "When you vote for Trump, it's almost giving the middle finger to the establishment or the status quo."[36] Another respondent stated, "Most of all we are Republicans who need change, and he is our man to get the job done."[37] Trump supporters have also learned his aggressive tactics and have become increasingly more aggressive online. Fifty-seven percent of people surveyed said Trump supporters are "very aggressive and/ or threatening online." Thirty-five percent of self-identified Trump supporters agreed with this statement.[38] As Allyson Kapin of the RAD Campaign that administered the survey stated, "We were noticing . . . a rise in aggression and hostility online."[39]

The use of aggression as a means to take out frustration has become more acceptable among Trump supporters. When a team from the largely White Dallas Center-Grimes (DCG) school in West Des Moines, Iowa, lost in a 57–50 game to Perry High, a mostly Hispanic school, DCG students began chanting: "Trump, Trump!" The reference to his name gave them a feeling of dominance over the minority team, even though they were frustrated with the loss. As one of the Perry students stated: "It is a chant said to intimidate and discriminate our Latino/Hispanic students and it is a chant that is fueled by racism."[40] A similar incident happened between two Catholic schools in Merrillville, Indiana. When the mostly White Andrean High School lost in a 56–52 game to the predominantly Hispanic Bishop Noll, Andrean students lifted a large photo of Trump, along with a sign stating, "ESPN DEPORTES." Some of them also chanted: "Build a wall," while Bishop Noll students responded, "You're a racist!"[41]

Addressing Feelings of Deprivation

Perceptions of deprivation or disadvantage do not exist in a social vacuum. They are usually based on comparisons with other groups rather than on a simple view of the position of a group people belong to. The perception that one's own group has fewer resources or is in a lower position in comparison to other groups creates a feeling of deep dissatisfaction. People can compare their group with similar groups or with groups that have more socioeconomic or political advantages.[42] This comparison leads people to believe they are more discriminated against and underprivileged than others, and have fewer resources, rights, and opportunities than other groups.[43] The belief that the "grass is greener" on the other side is prevalent. This idea of being disadvantaged in comparison to other groups can be based in truth or, indeed, fantasy. Nevertheless, if people believe in it, this belief has a tendency to affect their behavior, making them strong supporters of social change.[44]

Moreover, this feeling of deprivation can also be reinforced through comparisons with the past. If people believe their current position is worse than before, their dissatisfaction with the current situation grows significantly. Further, if people predict a possible loss or have an expectation that their social and economic status could become even more desperate in the future, they feel even stronger relative deprivation.[45] Comparing the actual status of their group and expectations about its position, people feel offended by their lower status and, as a result, are strongly motivated to change the situation.

Trump shows a deep empathy with his supporters. "Republican candidates who can successfully portray themselves as at least as compassionate or empathetic as their opponents can turn a traditional Democratic advantage into an electoral asset."[46] Trump demonstrates to people he cares about them and shares in their frustrations.

Moreover, Trump reinforces the perception, prevalent among his White supporters, that they have fewer rights, resources, and capacities in comparison with other racial groups and in comparison with their previous position in American society. To address these feelings, he promotes the denial of certain protected class rights for African Americans and emphasizes the diminished position of his White supporters and their inclusive rights to regain the country.

White Republicans in the U.S. believe the current administration has systemically advanced the status of the African American population in comparison to Whites. Three-quarters of Republicans believe African Americans today do not experience racial discrimination.[47] However, almost half of White voters think there is discrimination against White people in the U.S. today, and 60 percent of White working-class Americans agree that discrimination against Whites has been increasing. In comparison with 2001, fewer White people believe they are better off than African Americans in terms of income, housing, and education. More than half of White voters stated that in 2015 it became harder for them to achieve the American Dream than in 2009; the number of White people who believe that it is *much* harder for them doubled from 2009 to 2015.[48] One of Trump's supporters referred to the discrimination against White Americans as "absolutely" real: "I mean, it seems like we really go overboard to make sure all these other nationalities nowadays and colors have their fair shake of it, but no one's looking out for the white guy anymore."[49]

This feeling of relative deprivation has deepened as a result of the economic recession, which resulted in an overall decline in income and a loss of jobs for many Americans. Among Whites, the perception of economic insecurity has led to more negative racial attitudes.[50] The financial crisis has also contributed to "the political rhetoric of the extreme right, which often attributes blame to minorities or foreigners."[51] White blue-collar workers, who were at the bottom of the income pyramid, were increasing their self-esteem by comparing themselves favorably to other racial groups. This comparison helped them feel positive about being at the top of the racial hierarchy, even if their financial standing was poor. For some of them, "more than simply 'change,' Obama's election felt like an *inversion*" that changed racial hierarchy.[52] As one Trump supporter stated,

> I think he's divided this country in many ways. I know in a lot of places in America there's a divide in color . . . like, when I walk up to someone in the stores I feel that they're wondering if I like them. . ... I didn't feel that before. I was accepting of everyone, and I hate that he brought that.[53]

This change in racial status has created a feeling of threat among White working-class Americans, which is fueled by a fear of becoming a social minority. "Making the changing national racial demographics salient led white Americans (regardless of political party affiliation) to endorse both race-related and relatively race-neutral conservative policy positions more strongly."[54] For many White working-class people,

> even a minimum amount of racial stress becomes intolerable, triggering a range of defensive moves. These moves include the outward display of emotions such as anger, fear, and guilt, and behaviors such as argumentation, silence, and leaving the stress-inducing situation. These behaviors, in turn, function to reinstate white racial equilibrium.[55]

Consequently, many White voters want to see a restoration of the strict racial hierarchy that once existed so visibly in the U.S. Seventy percent of Trump voters in South Carolina wish the Confederate battle flag was still flying on their statehouse grounds.[56]

As these feelings of relative deprivation severely impact White workers and lead to an increase in their biases, they have become stigmatized by society as prejudiced racists. There are no specific policies that address the needs of this population and, as a result, they feel disfranchised from the political and social life of the nation. As one Republican donor said, "Republicans and Democrats alike had neglected the people who truly make our country work—the truck drivers, farmers, welders, hospitality workers."[57] Stigmatization only contributes to their resentment.

Trump has been able to capitalize on this bitterness, echoing the same prejudicial views regarding race and racial relations. Referring to the African American youth, Trump noted they had reached "a point where they've just about never done more poorly, there's no spirit, there's killings on an hourly basis virtually in places like Baltimore and Chicago and many other places."[58] This statement resonates with the sentiments of his voters who believe "blacks could be just as well off as whites if they only tried harder."[59] Trump has also criticized Obama for exclusively promoting the agenda of African Americans: "I thought that President Obama would be a great cheerleader for the country. And he's really become very divisive."[60] He also tweeted, "Our great African American President hasn't exactly had a positive impact on the thugs who are so happily and openly destroying Baltimore!"[61]

Not surprisingly, White voters with higher levels of racial resentment show greater support for Trump.[62] As one supporter stated, "White Americans founded this country. We are being pushed aside because of the President's administration and the media."[63] Another supporter echoed this sentiment, referring to the Black Lives Matter movement: "All lives matter. You know this is bulls—about black lives matter—doesn't all lives matter?"[64] They support Trump because they believe he understands the situation and can bring about change: "He gets it. We've sold ourselves out."[65]

Feeding Perceptions of Threat

To mirror the feelings of frustration and relative deprivation among his supporters, Trump has effectively employed a strategy premised on threats to
the U.S. The term "threat" always points to something that is a source of
danger, with its intended result to inflict harm on others. It stresses a potential
source of danger associated with certain activities and the ability or intent of
a threat agent to adversely affect a specific target. Thus if danger describes a
situation, threat shows the vector of intention from the source to its target; it
always stresses harm. Emphasizing outgroup threat, Trump cites negative or
aggressive intentions aimed directly toward his supporters. No matter if this
threat is real or perceived—it always affects the behavior of in-group members.[66] The feeling of group threats lead to more hostility toward opposing
groups, which helps Trump to justify the unfavorable treatment of opposing
groups and, thus, gain more support from his followers. For example, Trump
has employed several types of perceived threats to reinforce prejudice toward
immigrants, including perceived job losses and increased social assistance
to immigrants. As we have seen, Trump presents immigrants as limiting the
socioeconomic opportunities of American workers.

Perceptions of threat are also connected to the attribution of goals and
intentions to others. People typically attribute negative rather than positive
attitudes and goals to others,[67] connecting them to political extremism, violence, and nationalism.[68] Trump builds on the perception of Syrian refugees
as a threat to the U.S. and has described them in terms of their harmful and
aggressive motivation and goals. Eighty percent of Americans say ISIS is a
major threat to the well-being of the U.S.[69] Many people connect the threat
of ISIS with Syrian refugees. Thus 85 percent of Trump supporters see the
refugees fleeing the Islamic State militant group as a threat.[70]

Trump supports these feelings of threat and justifies them for his supporters. He stresses that the current system is not equipped to clearly identify the
refugees and protect the country from possible terrorists. He is comparing
this situation to the legend of the Trojan horse, emphasizing the covert nature
of Islamic terrorism. He stated, "We have no idea who these people are, we
are the worst when it comes to paperwork. This could be one of the great
Trojan horses."[71] Later he added, "I've talked to the greatest legal people,
spoken to the greatest security people. There's absolutely no way of saying
where these people come from. They may be from Syria, they may be ISIS,
they may be ISIS related."[72] At a rally in Washington state, he stated,

> Syrian refugees are on their way to this state. These people are totally
> undocumented. There's no proof. They have no paperwork. Nobody
> knows where the h**l they come . . . More than 90 percent of the recent
> refugees from the Middle East receive welfare.[73]

He added that U.S. citizens should not have to carry such a burden and rather the neighboring Gulf states should pay to create safe havens for refugees.

Trump connects Syrian refugees to terrorism, warning of inevitable attacks on U.S. soil. At one rally he stated,

> You know you saw what happened in Paris. You saw what happened at the World Trade Center. You saw what happened in California with the 14 people that they worked with, shot, killed, many people in the hospital. These are people that nobody knows who they are. And they're gonna be in your community. You can't do it.[74]

Speaking on a podcast hosted by the National Border Patrol Council, he emphasized the certainty of attacks: "Bad things will happen. A lot of bad things will happen. There will be attacks that you wouldn't believe. There will be attacks by the people that are right now coming into our country."[75] Regarding Syrian refugees entering the U.S., Trump has proposed a "closed door" strategy in order to prevent potential terrorist actions:

> We would be very, very strict. We would be very vigilant. And frankly, the easiest way to solve the problem—and it's gonna be a big problem if they keep doing this, and it already is a big problem—is to just not let it happen.[76]

In another speech, Trump added, "We cannot let them into this country, period. Our country has tremendous problems. We can't have another problem."[77]

Trump supporters have strongly approved of his position on immigration and refugees. As some of his supporters stated, "He is right, the Syrian refugees don't care about this country." "These invaders are on a mission to wreak havoc on Christian nations and our politicians are selling us out to them," and "Keep America Islam-free."[78] The crowd cheered when Trump said he could tell Syrian children that they couldn't go to school: "I can look in their faces and say, 'You can't come here.'"[79]

Creating Vanities

Arrogance and a lack of empathy for others are typical of behavior associated with narcissistic personality types. Narcissists desire personal admiration in addition to admiration of their achievements. Some psychologists believe Trump's manipulative and demanding style of interaction with others, his cockiness and egocentrism represent typical narcissistic behavior.[80] Any diagnoses made from a distance are always speculative; however, Trump's behavior has the potential to be described as narcissistic. He uses every opportunity to promote himself:

> [Trump] repeats several times in the same conversation, he's already had three number-one bestsellers. Likewise, he is "running the biggest real-estate empire in the world" and he's "very competent and very rich," though "I don't want to toot my own horn."[81]

Trump has constantly stressed how great he is at making deals and running businesses, and how successful he has been at creating his empire. He is extremely proud of his apartment, presenting it as a symbol of the highest social status obtainable: "I show [my] apartment to very few people. Presidents. Kings."[82]

Trump has bragged about his hair, completely dismissing that it has become the butt of jokes and cartoons around the world. Speaking about hair, he has also used the opportunity to brag about his house, his car, his helicopter, his jet, and his business properties.

> The reason my hair looks so neat all the time is because I don't have to deal with the elements. I live in the building where I work. I take an elevator from my bedroom to my office. The rest of the time, I'm either in my stretch limousine, my private jet, my helicopter, or my private club in Palm Beach Florida.. .. If I happen to be outside, I'm probably on one of my golf courses, where I protect my hair from overexposure by wearing a golf hat.[83]

He even brags when he complains about awful traffic on the way to the airport: "Luckily, it was my plane we were heading to, my plane, so it's not as if I could have missed the flight."[84]

Trump's constant bragging about his business, his former model wife, and his life of extravagant wealth has not turned off many of his less than fortunate supporters. Instead, his supporters mirror his narcissism and feel better about themselves through this connection. By "sharing" narcissism with Trump, his supporters acquire a sense of self-importance and a feeling of entitlement. They believe through this connection to Trump they are perceived as high-status people who will receive favorable treatment from others. This connection also feeds their fantasies of access to unlimited success, power, brilliance, beauty, or glamour.

> Glamour generates a feeling of projection and longing: "if only." If only I could walk that red carpet, drive that car, wear that dress, belong to that group, have that job, be (or be with) that person. If only I could have that life.[85]

"Trump is the big time, the bright lights, the fancy everything—and wealth and fame and all things I am not but would like to be," says one of his supporters.[86] In 1996, Sarah Palin, then a commercial fisherman from Wasilla, Alaska, told reporters on her way to seeing the recently divorced Ivana, first wife of Trump, selling her new cosmetic line: "We want to see Ivana because we are so desperate in Alaska for any semblance of glamour and culture."[87] When Sarah Palin joined Donald Trump on the campaign trail in 2016, she was wearing a $700 Milly bolero, catching that sense of glamour she had dreamed of twenty years earlier.[88]

To create this sense of glamour, Trump has always aimed to have the most beautiful women around him. At boarding school, "He wasn't bringing the same girl. He had a variety of girls coming up. Donald was bringing in very pretty women, very sophisticated women and very well-dressed women."[89] Trump has continuously dated models and hired attractive employees. Throughout his campaign, he has constantly focused on his wife's beauty. In response to an anti-Trump super PAC, which posted a naked picture of his wife Melania taken during her modeling career, he posted another picture emphasizing the beauty of "Melania Trump." A split-screen meme included an unflattering photo of Mrs. Cruz beside a glamour shot of Melania. The meme contained the text, "No need to 'spill the beans' the images are worth a thousand words."[90] Trump supporters were particularly pleased with this comparison and did not disapprove of the idea of comparing candidates' wives. Moreover, a poll conducted by the *Times* showed 65 percent of people would feel angrier with someone if they posted a picture of their wife implying that she was unattractive versus 35 percent who would be more upset if the photo showed their wife as someone lacking class.[91]

Thus Trump not only feels connected to his supporters' views and positions but also empowers them through his aggressive actions, the denial of rights for others, and his narcissistic vanities. In the next chapter, we will explore how Trump helps his supporters define the world and understand the nation and society.

Notes

1. Barker, R., Dembo, T., and Lewin, K. "Frustration and aggression: An experiment with young children." *University of Iowa Studies in Child Welfare*, 18, (1941): 1–314.
2. Baron, R. A., and Richardson, D. R. *Human Aggression*. 2nd ed. New York: Plenum, 2004.
3. Melburg, V., and Tedeschi, J. "Displaced aggression: Frustration or impression management?" *European Journal of Social Psychology*, 19, no.2 (1989): 139–145.
4. Trump, Donald, *The Art of the Deal*. Mass Market Paperback, 2004.

5. Slack, Donovan. "Trump Bizarrely Links Cruz's Father to JFK Assassin: Cruz goes Ballistic," *USA TODAY*, May 3, 2016, accessed April 16, 2016 http://www.usatoday.com/story/news/politics/onpolitics/2016/05/03/trump-bizarrely-links-cruzs-father-jfk-assassin-cruz-goes-ballistic/83874972/
6. Recio, Maria. "Trump Links Cruz's Father to JFK Assassin, Channeling National Enquirer," *Miami Herald*, April 22, 2016, accessed April 22, 2016 http://www.miamiherald.com/news/politics-government/article73449297.html
7. Slack. "Trump Bizarrely Links Cruz's Father to JFK Assassin."
8. Ibid.
9. Trump, Donald Jr. "That was an impressive meltdown . . . Desperate but impressive. Reminded me of my 3 year old coming off a sugar high," *Twitter*, May 3, 2016, accessed April 16, 2016, https://mobile.twitter.com/DonaldJTrumpJr/status/727530864310161408
10. Ibid.
11. Fins, Antonio. "Trump Supporters Strike Back: A Timeline of Rally Confrontations," *Palm Beach Post*, March 29, 2016. April 17, 2016, http://www.palmbeachpost.com/news/news/national-govt-politics/tension-up-as-donald-trump-fans-fight-back-against/nqtq6/
12. Diamond, Jeremy. "Trump on Protester: 'Maybe He Should Have Been Roughed Up,'" *CNN*, November 23, 2015, accessed April 16, 2016, http://www.cnn.com/2015/11/22/politics/donald-trump-black-lives-matter-protester-confrontation/
13. Terkel, Amanda. "Donald Trump Says His Supporters 'Hit Back' at Protesters More Often," *Huffington Post*, March 11, 2016, accessed April 17, 2016, http://www.huffingtonpost.com/entry/donald-trump-protesters_us_56e2da10e4b0b25c918198c2
14. Stein, Sam, and Dana Liebelson. "Donald Trump Encourages Violence at His Rallies: His Fans Are Listening," *Huffington Post*, March 10, 2016, accessed April 17, 2016, http://www.huffingtonpost.com/entry/donald-trump-violence_us_56e1f16fe4b0b25c91815913
15. Trump, Melania. "Facebook Page," Facebook, *accessed* April 30, 2016, https://www.facebook.com/MelaniaTrump/
16. Golshan, Tara. "Julia Ioffe Profiled Melania Trump: Then She Started Getting Calls from Hitler," *Vox: Policy & Politics*, April 30, 2016, accessed April 30, 2016, http://www.vox.com/2016/4/30/11539078/melania-trump-gq-julia-ioffe-antisemitic-donald-Trump
17. Lind, Dara. "The Problem with Violence at Trump Rallies Starts with Trump Himself," *Vox: Policy & Politics*, March 13, 2016, accessed April 16, 2016, http://www.vox.com/2016/3/11/11202540/trump-violent
18. Obeidallah, Dean. "Why Won't Trump Denounce His Anti-Semitic Supporters?" *The Atlantic*, May 6, 2016, accessed May 7, 2016, http://www.theatlantic.com/politics/archive/2016/05/trump-needs-to-loudly-denounce-the-hate/481608/
19. Ross, Janell. "Donald Trump's Baffling Explanation for Violence at His Campaign Rallies," *The Washington Post*, March 11, 2016, accessed April 26, 2016, https://www.washingtonpost.com/news/the-fix/wp/2016/03/11/donald-trumps-baffling-explanation-for-violence-at-his-campaign-rallies/
20. Weiss, Rusty. "Donald Trump Gets Wind of Barack Obama's Comments about Him and Hists Back with THIS!" *Headline Politics*, accessed April 19, 2016, http://www.headlinepolitics.com/donald-trump-gets-wind-of-barack-obamas-comments-about-him-and-hits-back-with-this/
21. Charlton, Jordan. "Donald Trump Blasts President Obama: 'Worst President' in American History (Video)," *The Wrap*, July 28, 2015, accessed April 16, 2016,

http://www.thewrap.com/donald-trump-blasts-president-obama-worst-president-in-american-history-video/
22. Lee, M. J., Sara Murray, Jeremy Diamond, Noah Gray, and Tal Kopan. "Why I'm Voting for Trump," *CNN*, January 28, 2016, accessed April 17, 2016, http://www.cnn.com/2016/01/27/politics/donald-trump-voters-2016-election/
23. McElwee, Sean, and Jason McDaniel. "Some of Trump's Strongest Supporters Are Registered Democrats: Here's Why," *Salon*, March 5, 2016, accessed April 18, 2016, http://www.salon.com/2016/05/16/anatomy_of_a_donald_trump_supporter_what_really_motivates_this_terrifying_political_movement/
24. UIP. "Trump Says Another 9/11-Like Attack Likley If More Syrain Refugees Come to U.S.," *Breitbart*, May 16, 2016, accessed May 16, 2016, http://www.breitbart.com/news/trump-says-another-911-like-attack-likely-if-more-syrian-refugees-come-to-u-s/
25. Pedersen, W., Gonzales, C., and Miller, N. "The moderating effect of trivial triggering provocation on displaced aggression." *Journal of Personality and Social Psychology*, 78, no. 5 (2000): 913–927; Marcus-Newhall, A., Pedersen, W., Carlson, M., and Miller, N. (2000). "Displaced aggression is alive and well: A meta-analytic review." *Journal of Personality and Social Psychology*, 78, no. 4 (2000): 670–689.
26. Cooper, Betsy, Daniel Cox, Rachel Lienesch, and Robert P. Jones. "Anxiety, Nostalgia, and Mistrust: Finds from the 2015 American Values Survey," *PRRI*, November 17, 2015, accessed April 19, 2016, http://publicreligion.org/research/2015/11/survey-anxiety-nostalgia-and-mistrust-findings-from-the-2015-american-values-survey/#.Vzn6numKn8E
27. Lee, M. J., Sara Murray, Jeremy Diamond, Noah Gray, and Tal Kopan. "Why I'm Voting for Trump," *CNN*, January 28, 2016, accessed April 18, 2016, http://www.cnn.com/2016/01/27/politics/donald-trump-voters-2016-election/
28. Ibid.
29. Smith, Samantha. "Trump Supporters Differ from other GOP Voters on Foreign Policy, Immigration Issues," *Pew Research Center*, May 11, 2016, accessed May 12, 2016, http://www.pewresearch.org/fact-tank/2016/05/11/trump-supporters-differ-from-other-gop-voters-on-foreign-policy-immigration-issues/
30. Trump, Donald J. "Immigration Reform That Will Make American Great Again: The Three Core Principles of Donald J. Trump's Immigration Plan," *Trump: Make America Great Again!*, accessed April 19, 2016, https://www.donaldjtrump.com/positions/immigration-reform
31. Anderson, C.A., Bushman, B.J. "Human aggression." *Annual Review of Psychology* 53, no. 1 (2002): 27–51.
32. Kamisar, Ben. "Trump Brings Birther Charge against Cruz," *The Hill*, March 23, 2015, accessed April 19, 2016, http://thehill.com/blogs/ballot-box/236651-trump-cruz-faces-hurdle-for-canadian-birthplace
33. Richardson, Bradford. "Trump Supporters File 'Birther' Lawsuit against Cruz in Federal Court," *The Hill*, February 12, 2016, accessed April 18, 2016, http://thehill.com/blogs/ballot-box/presidential-races/269281-trump-supporters-file-federal-lawsuit-challenging-cruzs
34. Terkel, Amanda, and Sam Stein. "Donald Trump Accuses George W. Bush of Lying to Invade Iraq," *Huffington Post*, February 13, 2016, accessed April 20, 2016, http://www.huffingtonpost.com/entry/donald-trump-george-bush-iraq-invasion_us_56bfe8cbe4b0b40245c6f94b
35. Ibid.

36. Lee, M. J. "How Donald Trump Blasted George W. Bush in S.C.—and Still Won," *CNN*, February 21, 2016, accessed April 20, 2016, http://www.cnn.com/2016/02/20/politics/donald-trump-south-carolina-military/
37. Moons, Michelle. "Donald Trump: Illegal Immigration Costing Washington State Taxpayers $2.7 Billion," *Breitbart*, May 9, 2016, accessed May 16, 2016, http://www.breitbart.com/2016-presidential-race/2016/05/09/holdholdhold-donald-trump-illegal-immigration-costing-washington-state-taxpayers-2-7-billion/
38. "Is Social Media Empowering or Silencing Political Expression in the United States?" accessed May 29, 2016, http://onlineharassmentdata.org/2016elections/index.html
39. Gold, Hadas. "Survey: Donald Trump Supporters most Aggressive Online," *POLITO*, May 6, 2016, accessed May 17, 2016, http://www.politico.com/blogs/on-media/2016/05/survey-donald-trump-supporters-most-aggressive-online-222912#ixzz48O9Kbrvz
40. Associated Press. "Iowa Students Admonished for 'Trump!' Chants at Hoops Game," *Thonline*, February 26, 2016, accessed April 26, 2016, http://www.thonline.com/news/iowa-illinois-wisconsin/article_e488d0d2-dcc1-11e5-bf98-7f5dbe1314ad.html
41. Davich, Jerry. "Charges of Students' Hate Speech Puts School in the Penalty," *Post-Tribune*, February 28, 2016, accessed April 26, 2016, http://www.chicagotribune.com/suburbs/post-tribune/news/ct-ptb-davich-andrean-noll-trump-tactics-st-0229-20160228-story.html
42. Runciman, Walter Garrison. *Relative Deprivation and Social Justice: A Study of Attitudes to Social Inequality in Twentiety-Century England.* California: University of California, 1966.
43. Faye Crosby. "The denial of personal discrimination." *American Behavioral Scientist* 27, no. 3 (1984): 371–386.
44. Kawakami, Kerry, and Kenneth L. Dion. "The Impact of Salient Self-Identities on Relative Deprivation and Action Intentions." *European Journal of Social Psychology* 23, no. 5 (1993): 525–540; Walker, Iain and Thomas F. Pettigrew. "Relative Deprivation Theory: An Overview and Conceptual Critique." *British Journal of Social Psychology*, 23, no. 4 (1984): 301–310.
45. Davis, J. A. "A formal interpretation of the theory of relative deprivation." *Sociometry* 22 (1959): 280–296; Runciman, W. G. *Relative Deprivation and Social Justice: A Study of Attitudes to Social Inequality in Twentieth Century England.* Penguin Books Ltd., 1972; Tanter, Raymond, and Ted R. Gurr. "Why men rebel." *Midwest Journal of Political Science* 14, no. 4, (1970): 725.
46. Nyhan, Brendan. "Why Republicans Are Suddenly Talking about Economic Inequality," *New York Times*, February 13, 2015, accessed April 13, 2016, http://www.nytimes.com/2015/02/14/upshot/why-republicans-are-suddenly-talking-about-economic-inequality.html?abt=0002&abg=1&_r=0
47. Cooper, Betsy, Daniel Cox, Rachel Lienesch, and Robert P. Jones. "Anxiety, Nostalgia, and Mistrust: Finds from the 2015 American Values Survey," *PRRI*, November 17, 2015, accessed April 12, 2016, http://publicreligion.org/research/2015/11/survey-anxiety-nostalgia-and-mistrust-findings-from-the-2015-american-values-survey/#.Vzn6numKn8E
48. CNN/Kaiser Family Foundation. "Survey of Americans on Race," *CNN/Kaiser Family Foundation*, November 2015, accessed April 12, 2016, https://assets.documentcloud.org/documents/2600623/kff-cnn-race-topline-final.pdf

49. Lee, M. J., Sara Murray, Jeremy Diamond, Noah Gray, and Tal Kopan. "Why I'm Voting for Trump," *CNN*, January 28, 2016, accessed April 12, 2016, http://www.cnn.com/2016/01/27/politics/donald-trump-voters-2016-election/

50. McElwee, Sean, and Jason McDaniel. "Some of Trump's Strongest Supporters Are Registered Democrats. Here's Why," *Salon*, March 5, 2016, accessed April 16, 2016, http://www.salon.com/2016/03/05/some_of_trumps_strongest_supporters_are_registered_democrats_heres_why/

51. Funke, Manuel, Moritz Schularick, and Christophe Trebesch. "Going to Extremes: Politics after Financial Crisis, 1870–2014," *CESifo Working Paper No. 5553, Category 7: Monetary Policy and International Finance*, October 2015, accessed April 14, 2016, http://www.statewatch.org/news/2015/oct/financial-crises-cesifo-wp-5553.pdf

52. Bouie, "How Trump Happened."

53. Ibid.

54. Craig, Maureen A., and Jennifer A. Richeson. "On the precipice of a 'majority-minority' America: Perceived status threat from the racial demographic shift affects White Americans' political ideology." *Psychological Science*, 2014 25, pp. 1189–1197.

55. Di'Angelo, Robin. "White Fragility." *The International Journal of Critical Pedagogy*, 3, no. 3 (2011) pp 54–70.

56. Vavreck, Lynn. "Measuring Donald Trump's Supporters for Intolerance," *New York Times*, February 23, 2016, accessed April 29, 2016, http://www.nytimes.com/2016/02/25/upshot/measuring-donald-trumps-supporters-for-intolerance.html?_r=0

57. Confessore, Nicholas. "How the G.O.P Elite Lost its Voters to Donald Trump," *New York Times*, March 28, 2016, accessed April 2, 2016, http://www.nytimes.com/2016/03/28/us/politics/donald-trump-republican-voters.html?_r=1

58. Moodley, Kiran. "Donald Trump Says African-American Youths 'Have No Spirit,'" *Independent*, June 24, 2015, accessed April 6, 2016, http://www.independent.co.uk/news/people/donald-trump-says-african-american-youths-have-no-spirit-10342030.html

59. RAND American Life Panel, RAND Corporation, accessed April 18, 2016, http://www.rand.org/pubs/corporate_pubs/CP508-2015–05.html

60. Moodley, "Donald Trump Says African-American Youths 'Have No Spirit.'"

61. Trump, Donald J. "Our great African American President hasn't exactly had a positive impact on the thugs who are so happily and openly destroying Baltimore," *Twitter*, April 27, 2016, accessed April 27, 2016, https://mobile.twitter.com/realDonaldTrump/status/592910662424223744

62. McDaniel, Jason. "Racial resentment increases support for Trump, but not for Rubio. Created with newly released data from ANES 2016," *Twitter*, March 5, 2016, accessed April 14, 2016, https://mobile.twitter.com/ValisJason/status/706285257121624064

63. Lee, M. J., Sara Murray, Jeremy Diamond, Noah Gray, and Tal Kopan. "Why I'm Voting for Trump," *CNN*, January 28, 2016, accessed April 7, 2016, http://www.cnn.com/2016/01/27/politics/donald-trump-voters-2016-election/

64. Ibid.

65. Confessore, "How the G.O.P Elite Lost Its Voters to Donald Trump."

66. Harré, Rom, and Luk Van Langenhove, eds. *Positioning Theory: Moral Contexts of International Action*. 1st ed. Wiley-Blackwell, 1998, 5–347.

67. Heider, Fritz. *The Psychology of Interpersonal Relations*. New York: Wiley, 1958.

68. Hagendoorn, L., Csepeli, G., Dekker, H., and Farnen, R. *European Nations and Nationalism: Theoretical and Historical Perspectives.* Aldershot: Ashgate, 2000.
69. Pew Research Center Staff. "Public Uncertain, Divided Over America's Place in the World."
70. Ali, Idrees. "Trump Supporters See Iraqi, Syrian Refugees as Major Threat: Report," *Reuters*, May 5, 2016, accessed May 5, 2016, http://www.reuters.com/article/us-usa-election-trump-refugees-idUSKCN0XW095
71. Kopan, Tal. "Donald Trump: Syrian Refugees a 'Trojan Horse," *CNN*, November 16, 2015, accessed April 12, 2016, http://www.cnn.com/2015/11/16/politics/donald-trump-syrian-refugees/
72. Kamisar, Ben. "Trump to Syrian Refugee Children" 'You Can't Come Here,'" *The Hill*, February 8, 2016, accessed April 13, 2016 http://thehill.com/blogs/ballot-box/gop-primaries/268614-trump-to-syrian-refugee-children-you-cant-come-here
73. Moons, Michelle. "Donald Trump: Illegal Immigration Costing Washington State Taxpayers $2.7 Billion," *Breitbart*, May 9, 2016, accessed May 9, 2016, http://www.breitbart.com/2016-presidential-race/2016/05/09/holdholdhold-donald-trump-illegal-immigration-costing-washington-state-taxpayers-2–7-billion/
74. Ibid.
75. Martosko, David. "'There Will Be Attacks That You Wouldn't Believe': Trump Warns Border Patrol Agents that Syrian Refugees will Bring Islamist Terror with them," *Daily Mail*, May 16, 2016, accessed May 17, 2016, http://www.dailymail.co.uk/news/article-3593233/There-attacks-wouldn-t-believe-Trump-warns-border-patrol-agents-Syrian-refugees-cause-9–11.html#ixzz48wGSWDRG
76. Ibid.
77. Kopan, "Donald Trump: Syrian Refugees a 'Trojan horse'."
78. UIP. "Trump Says Another 9/11-Like Attack Likley If More Syrian Refugees Come to U.S.," *Breitbart*, May 16, 2016, accessed May 17, 2016, http://www.breitbart.com/news/trump-says-another-911-like-attack-likely-if-more-syrian-refugees-come-to-u-s/
79. Kamisar, "Trump to Syrian Refugee Children."
80. , Henry. "Is Donald Trump Actually A Narcissist? Therapists Weigh In!" *Vanity Fair*, November 11, 2015, accessed April 15, 2016, http://www.vanityfair.com/news/2015/11/donald-trump-narcissism-therapists
81. Swogger, Glenn, Jr., and Henry I. Miller. "Donald Trump: Narcissist-In-Chief, Not Commander-In-Chief," *Forbes*, March 30, 2016, accessed April 4, 2016, http://www.forbes.com/sites/realspin/2016/03/30/donald-trump-narcissist-in-chief-not-commander-in-chief/#2d0279765595
82. Blair, Gwenda. *Donald Trump: Master Apprentice.* Simon and Schuster, 2005: 222.
83. Trump, Donald J., and Meredith McIver. *Trump: How to Get Rich.* Ballantine Books, 2004:152.
84. Lozada, Carlos. "I Just Binge-Read Eight Books by Donald Trump. Here's What I Learned," *The Washington Post*, July 30, 2015, accessed April 5, 2016, https://www.washingtonpost.com/news/book-party/wp/2015/07/30/i-just-binge-read-eight-books-by-donald-trump-heres-what-i-learned/
85. Postrel, Virginia. "Trump Isn't Just Campaigning. He's Selling His Supporters a Glamorous Life," *The Washington Post*, March 18, 2016, accessed April 6, 2016, https://www.washingtonpost.com/opinions/trump-is-selling-a-dream-his-supporters-are-buying/2016/03/18/5307698e-eb8f-11e5-bc08–3e03a5b41910_story.html

86. Ibid.
87. Bell, Tom. "Alaskans Line Up for a Whiff of Ivana," *Alaska Dispatch News*, April 3, 1996, accessed April 4, 2016, http://www.adn.com/article/19960403/alaskans-line-whiff-ivana
88. Parry, Hannah. "Sarah Palin Wore $700 Decorative Bolero as She Joined Donald Trump\s Presidential Campaign," *Daily Mail*, January 20, 2016, accessed April 4, 2016, http://www.dailymail.co.uk/news/article-3409224/Sarah-Palin-wore-700-decorative-bolero-joined-Donald-Trump-s-presidential-campaign.html
89. Barbaro, Michael, and Megan Twohey. "Crossing the Line: How Donald Trump Behaved with Women in Private," *New York times*, May 14, 2016, accessed May 14, 2016, http://www.nytimes.com/2016/05/15/us/politics/donald-trump-women.html?hp&action=click&pgtype=Homepage&clickSource=story-heading&module=first-column-region&region=top-news&WT.nav=top-news&_r=1
90. Kimble, Lindsey. "Doubling Down, Donald Trump Tweets a My-Wife's-Prettier-Than Yours Meme Featuring Heidi Cruz—and Ted Fires Back," *People*, March 24, 2016, accessed April 14, 2016, http://www.people.com/article/donald-trump-posts-meme-of-heidi-cruz
91. April 11, 2016 issue of *Time*.

5   The World Is Simple

People are typically uncomfortable with the complexity of social reality. In order to make sense of the multifaceted aspects of society, they use a method of "mini-max": using minimal effort for maximum effect. People prefer simple, lucid stories about society and the world in which they live, opting for easy-to-understand descriptions of the nation and the problems facing it. Trump helps to simplify how his supporters perceive social reality by employing several mechanisms, including stereotyping and cognitive dissonance, reducing uncertainty and ambiguity, addressing ambivalence, and confirming their biases.

Stereotyping

The complex narratives surrounding the history of a nation and a society are generally underpinned by both concrete and stable sets of symbols,[1] in addition to basic ideas that help construct new ideologies or challenge existing ones.[2] These sets of symbols usually offer a point of comparison and provide simple meanings, which help people digest complex information.[3] Complex social processes are, thus, transformed into stories capturing the gist of social realities in a simplistic manner.[4] One of the core mechanisms that reduce a person's need to analyze and process complex information is stereotyping. Through stereotypes, we simplify our social world by creating shared ideas about the characteristics of specific people and different groups. Most stereotypes tend to convey a less favorable impression of others, recreating "us-versus-them" perceptions.

Trump has been actively using stereotypes to describe particular people and groups. He describes his opponents by labeling them in simple yet memorably unfavorable terms. These labels are easy for people to remember, and they provide stability and certainty. The elementary nature of these labels strongly affects people's perceptions. They work as powerful monikers that create long-lasting impressions. People begin to use these memorable markers to describe particular individuals, while simultaneously denying all their other features.

During the GOP debates hosted by Fox News, Trump referred to presidential hopeful Marco Rubio as "Little Marco:" "Don't worry about it, Marco. Don't worry about it, Little Marco, I will."[5] By doing so, Trump created a facile label for Marco Rubio that his supporters could latch on to, which they did. This label became instantly popular online.[6] Trump supporters filled the Internet with a photo of Marco Rubio taken on August 26, 2015, while visiting a furniture store in Franklin, New Hampshire. The photo showed Rubio sitting in a gigantic chair. Trump supporters also created several Little Marco memes, depicting him as a child and posting comments such as, "When you tell everyone you'd stay in the race, but then mom calls you downstairs for dinner."[7] Some memes presented Trump as a father and Rubio as a toddler. Created against the backdrop of the initial, Trump-inspired label "Little Marco," these depictions of Marco Rubio had the effect of generating an image of Marco Rubio as a junior politician not capable of assuming the position of president and running the country.

Trump also created the label "Lying Ted" for Ted Cruz. Trump first used this identifier during a rally in Columbus, Ohio on Super Tuesday: "I call him 'Lying Ted.' The only advantage I have is I have a big speaker out there. We don't have to lie."[8] Trump methodically connected the name of Cruz with someone who lies. At the GOP debate hosted by Fox News, he responded to Cruz's accusations that he had been deceiving people about his position on immigration: "You're the lying guy up here. You're the one, you're the one . . . I've given my answer, Lying Ted. I've given my answer."[9] Trump has continuously used this label at his rallies: "In the case of Lyin' Ted Cruz. Lyin' Ted. Lies. Ooh, he lies. You know Ted. He brings the Bible, holds it high, puts it down, lies."[10]

Trump supporters have actively reinforced this notion of Ted Cruz as a liar. In Indiana, Trump supporters did not shake Cruz's hand, calling him Lying Ted to his face.[11] This negative label has proven to be extremely powerful and has inspired several investigations, which have been led by Trump supporters themselves. For example, when Ted Cruz stated he simply did not know former Speaker of the House, John Boehner, who had directly compared him to Satan,[12] an investigation showed Cruz once worked as Boehner's lawyer. The website reinforced the notion of Cruz as a liar: "It seems overwhelmingly likely that, given the fact that Ted Cruz worked as John Boehner's lawyer, he has 'worked' with him, and almost certainly does 'know' him."[13] By creating the label "Lying Ted," Trump created an effective tool that successfully branded Ted Cruz as dishonest and untrustworthy among Trump would-be supporters.

Trump heavily relied on creating labels for his fellow GOP presidential hopefuls. Trump also labeled Democratic presidential hopeful Hilary Clinton

"Crooked Hillary" at a rally in Watertown, New York: "I'm not controlled by the special interests, by the lobbyists. They control Crooked Hillary."[14] Explaining why he was using this label, Trump told Fox News: "I will tell you, the word 'Crooked Hillary' is 100 percent correct."[15] As evidence, Trump cited several high profile incidents: the Whitewater scandal in the 1980s concerning loans for real estate in Arkansas that contributed to a collapse of a local savings and loan, Clinton's use of a private e-mail server for classified information, and the Clinton Foundation's questionable funding sources tied to foreign entities, in addition to Clinton's acceptance of millions of dollars for speeches at private financial organizations. Emphasizing her inconsistency on women's rights, Trump tweeted, "How can Crooked Hillary say she cares about women when she is silent on radical Islam, which horribly oppresses women?"[16] Addressing Clinton's position on gun control, Trump stated, "Crooked Hillary wants to get rid of all guns and yet she is surrounded by bodyguards who are fully armed. No more guns to protect Hillary!"[17] Building on the Rasmussen poll, which showed only 4 percent of American women support Clinton's Middle East migration proposal,[18] Trump aggressively stated, "Crooked Hillary Clinton overregulates, overtaxes and doesn't care about jobs. Most importantly, she suffers from plain old bad judgment!"[19] In addition to labeling Clinton as dishonest, Trump presented both Clinton and her entire presidential campaign as "crooked." On *Fox and Friends*, he stated, "I call her 'Crooked Hillary' because she's crooked, and you know the only thing she's got is the woman card."[20] His supporters have employed this label with great satisfaction: "She is a crook using woman card to deceive people. Expose her."[21] This label has had the effect of encouraging people to search for more examples of Clinton's dishonesty. Nearly half of all supporters of Trump have stated that they support him because they "don't want Hillary Clinton to win."[22]

Trump has also capitalized on stereotypes about social groups to explain the world. He has referred to Mexicans crossing the U.S.-Mexico border illegally into the U.S. as "rapists" and "criminals," whereas Hispanics in general were referred to as "incredible workers." His supporters readily accept these stereotypes because they are not only memorable in a pejorative way but they also define social reality. His supporters "feed" on the simplification produced by Trump through stereotypes and labeling, and they, in turn, feel more confident in their understanding of the world.

Need for Certainty

People actively seek to reduce uncertainty. Uncertainty is usually experienced as an unpleasant and frustrating sentiment. As a result, people are highly motivated to create more certainty in how they see the world.[23] Many people even have an inability to tolerate any uncertainty because such feelings make them anxious and worried about themselves and the world around them.[24] To deal with such uncertainty, people seek to employ passive strategies of observation or active strategies seeking specific information. Trump provides an easy alternative to these strategies: he, himself, reduces uncertainty for his supporters. And they appreciate the luxury of a clear and defined world, which they perceive Trump provides.

People who have a strong need for simple order and stability typically prefer politicians who use more nouns in their speeches. For such individuals, it is easier to understand descriptions of people or events through their permanent characteristics rather than comprehending relativity or transformations. Trump provides this certainty in his speeches, describing particular situations and people in simple terms: "I'm really rich"; "Politicians are all talk, no action"; H1B visa is "very, very bad for workers."[25] His assessments are also rather limited to several adjectives such as "nice," "huge," "terrible," "beautiful."

Trump avoids contradictions and addresses every issue with "tremendous self-confidence and 100 percent certainty, which some people find impressive and reassuring."[26] In a few short sentences, he has an uncanny ability to present the major problems facing the U.S., which are typically framed in hyperbolic terms. Although Trump promises to address these issues, he does so without providing any specific details. For example,

> We've lost our jobs. We've lost everything. We're losing everything. Our jobs are gone, our businesses are being taken out of the country. I want to make America great again and I want to leave Social Security as is. We're going to get rid of waste, fraud, abuse, and bring back business.[27]

Speaking about the threat of Islam, Trump also provides a simplistic description: "I will tell you this. There's something going on that maybe you don't know about, maybe a lot of other people don't know about, but there's tremendous hatred." [28]

Trump has continually opted for a straightforward approach couched in plain and simple English:

> It is the kind of thinking our country needs—understanding how to get a good result out of a very bad and sad situation. Politicians have no idea how to do this—they don't have a clue. I will create jobs, bring back companies and not make it easy for companies to leave.[29]

His supporters perceive his accounts and promises as essential and incontestable and, thus, enjoy a high degree of sureness of the social reality Trump is claiming he will be able to provide. They gladly buy the simplicity of his answers: "The guy is the real thing. He says what he believes, and you know where he stands."[30]

Ambiguity creates similarly unpleasant feelings and can be threatening for many people.[31] Ambiguous positions and statements lead to vagueness and confusion. Faced with ambiguity, people experience a need for closure. They prefer quick, decisive answers. They also have a need to create and maintain simpler, unambiguous explanations, thus receiving specific closure.[32] Trump provides for this need for closure by offering simple and seemingly straightforward answers and therefore formulating easy resolutions to complex socio-political problems.

Trump's populism, therefore, is a form of connection to the American electorate rather than to an ideology. He provides certainty in simple answers and solutions to difficult problems. He addresses peoples' worries derived from uncertainties about jobs. Although government figures point to the fact that the unemployment rate in the U.S. is down to 5 percent, this does not reflect the everyday reality of blue-collar workers. People are frustrated because the absence of well-paying jobs is forcing them to take on two or three minimum wage jobs; many workers have stopped looking for work or are working at jobs beneath their skill set. Moreover, with fewer full-time jobs, many temporary or part-time workers are receiving no medical or retirement benefits. Today, American households earn about the same as they did twenty years ago, adjusted to inflation, which has meant people are struggling more and more to make ends meet—when accounting for rising cost of medical, education, and training costs.[33] The participation rate for White men in the workforce has steadily declined over the past six decades: 72 percent now from 88 percent in 1954.[34] Sixty-seven percent of Americans believe the country is on the wrong track, whereas only 27 percent think it is going in the right direction.[35] As one Trump supporter stated, "The American worker is being left behind." Another supporter echoed this sentiment, noting, "An awful lot of us in the middle class are losing our shirts."[36]

Trump's main message to people has continually been that career politicians have betrayed the American working and middle classes to maximize profit for themselves and wealthy corporations. Trump has suggested that the notion of the American Dream is dead and the country is no longer great: "This country is dying. And our workers are losing their jobs."[37] As such, Trump has promised to reverse the situation completely by bringing jobs back to the U.S. and protecting American workers. He has offered both staunch and potential supporters an easy to understand and decisive approach: "We're gonna fix it." He has guaranteed simple solutions: bring back jobs from China, Japan, and Mexico and renegotiate "trade pacts that are no good for us and no good for our workers."[38] Building on protectionist sentiments, Trump has promised to restrict immigration and build a wall. During complex discussions on health care, Trump has proposed the need to provide universal health coverage for everyone. Among his supporters, he has successfully created an impression of himself as a difference maker, capable of handling any and every problem facing America: he will resolve all their problems—just let him handle it.

According to the theory of conformism, people who have problems making decisions or taking a position on an issue, especially in a situation of crisis or uncertainty, leave decision making to the group and its leadership. By attaching themselves to Trump as a leader and seeing his supporters as a reference group, many people join by accepting the particular beliefs and positions of the group.[39] The majority of Trump's solutions may seem like overpromising, but they are easy to understand and support. Trump supporters from varying socioeconomic backgrounds see him as the long awaited answer to the entrenched problems in the country. They are attracted to his populist rhetoric and feel more comfortable with Trump than they do with traditional career politicians. As Robert Reich notes,

> A Latina-American from Laredo, Texas, tells me she and most of her friends are for Trump because he wants to keep Mexicans out. She thinks too many Mexicans have come here illegally, making it harder for those here legally. A union member from Pittsburgh says he's for Trump because he'll be tough on American companies shipping jobs abroad, tough with the Chinese, tough with Muslims. A small businessman in Cincinnati tells me he's for Trump because "Trump's not a politician. He'll give them hell in Washington."[40]

These accounts demonstrate how effective Trump's simple yet memorable messages are in reducing people's anxiety about the current political and social uncertainty. These messages also provide them with the closure they so desperately need.

Crossing the Boundary

Another cognitive phenomenon making people uncomfortable is ambivalence-uncertainty or fluctuation, especially when people have a hard time making choices. When people feel frustrated, they also have a simultaneous desire to say or do two opposite or conflicting things at the same time. It is hard to make decisions or choose particular positions because both of them reflect certain values that are important to that person. The annoyance of indecision can lead to even more stress.

Ambivalence is a common phenomenon in the world of politics. Political parties and candidates typically focus on specific issues, which have historically been winning party issues. For example, Democratic presidential candidates have traditionally addressed issues dealing with education and health care, whereas Republicans are typically perceived as the better party to address crime and national security.[41] The Republican Party line had clearly defined differences in positions toward abortion, taxation, universal health care, and workers unions. It promotes pro-life values, policies of cutting taxes, reducing welfare programs, limiting the power of workers' unions, and immigration. The Republican Party prioritizes economic growth and budget austerity over welfare and entitlements.

However, people very rarely (only about 20 percent of voters) are consistent in their views as liberal or conservative.[42] For most people, their position on one issue does not predict their attitude toward other issues. Around a quarter of voters in the U.S. identify themselves as conservatives but often take liberal positions regarding issues such as the size of the government.[43] Many Republicans feel uneasy about their belonging to a political party when their beliefs about particular issues are not reflective of the party position. Within the Republican Party, which aims to decrease the entitlement budget, only 21 percent favored cuts in Medicare and only 17 percent wanted to see spending on Social Security reduced. Almost 30 percent of Republicans would welcome "heavy" taxes on the wealthy,[44] and only 36 percent want to cut aid to the poor.[45] Such ambivalent attitudes are more susceptible to information or persuasion by the candidate that straddles different positions.[46]

As a Republican candidate, Trump actively blurs these party lines by supporting issues that have been traditionally associated with the Democratic Party, including health care, workers' unions, and education. When Trump was asked about three main functions of the government, he advocated for one conventionally Republican issue and two issues traditionally promoted by the Democrats: "Well, the greatest function of all by far is security for our nation. I would also say health care; I would also say education."[47] By cutting across the political divide, Trump emphasizes that his approach still falls within the Republican Party. He compares himself to former president Ronald Reagan:

> Ronald Reagan signed one of the toughest abortion laws in favor of abortion in California that had been signed in many, many years. And yet he was a great president and a—pretty conservative—he wasn't very conservative, but he was a pretty conservative president.[48]

Trump not only promises to maintain Medicare and Social Security but he is also sympathetic to rolling out a new form of universal health care that would be different from Obamacare: "You can't have a guy that has no money, that's sick, and he can't go see a doctor, he can't go see a hospital . . . you have to take care of poor people."[49] Trump has promised to protect pensions from policies promoted by rivals in his own party:

> We've got Social Security that's going to be destroyed if somebody like me doesn't bring money into the country. All these other people want to cut the hell out of it. I'm not going to cut it at all; I'm going to bring money in, and we're going to save it.[50]

He has promised to keep the Social Security program intact: "I will do everything within my power not to touch Social Security, to leave it the way it is; to make this country rich again."[51] This position makes him much more popular among Republican voters than any of the other candidates who promote cuts in social spending: "Trump's defense of federal retirement programs aligns him with his voters and against the fervent desires of Republican insiders."[52] Consequently, Trump has done significantly better among voters who want spending increased rather than decreased and winning over conflicted conservatives.[53]

Trump successfully caters to people who want to maintain or increase spending on Social Security and who support a decrease in immigration because of his strong stance on both. "So when Trump speaks out against both immigration and against fellow Republicans who want to cut Social Security, he's speaking out for a lot of people."[54] These people, around 40 percent of the U.S. population, were left behind by candidates who followed party lines strictly.

At numerous occasions during his campaign trail speeches, Trump has claimed he was against the war in Iraq from the very start: "You know, I was against the war in Iraq. I said you shouldn't go in. You're going to destabilize the Middle East. I was so strong against Iraq,"[55] "And, I was against the war in Iraq. OK? I am not a fast trigger. I'm exactly the opposite of that. We should have never gone in, it destabilized the Middle East."[56] "I said don't go into Iraq even though I'm a very militaristic person."[57] The record shows that Trump did express support for the war in Iraq in 2002.[58] In 2004, however, he actively criticized the invasion:

> What was the purpose of this whole thing? Hundreds and hundreds of young people killed. And what about the people coming back with no arms and legs? Not to mention the other side. All those Iraqi kids who've been blown to pieces. And it turns out that all of the reasons for the war were blatantly wrong. All this for nothing![59]

This deviation from the established party line on the Iraq War has positively resonated with Trump's supporters and provides them with cognitive certainty and liberation. As one supporter noted, he felt "liberated" when Trump called George W. Bush a liar regarding the false premise for the Iraq War: "We knew the war was wrong but we're loyal Republicans and we couldn't say it."[60]

Trump has also attracted several Democratic voters who have been skeptical of the authenticity of the Democratic Party and are ready to cross the political boundary. About 20 percent of likely Democratic voters say they would vote for Trump.[61] This figure includes, in addition to Whites, African American and some Hispanic voters. In Ohio, for example, Trump managed to secure 15 percent of their support.[62] Trump showed himself to be a supporter of unionized labor. In *The America We Deserve*, he stated, "Unions still have a place in American society. In fact, with the globalization craze in full heat, unions are about the only political force reminding us to remember the American working family."[63] Even his fight with a Las Vegas union over the contact for his hotel has not discouraged his supporters. A study of worker voting preferences in Cleveland and Pittsburgh showed that 25 percent of Democrats strongly support Trump.[64] As Karen Nussbaum, executive director of Working America has described,

> We hear the same refrains all the time. That people are fed up and they're hurting. That their families have not recovered from the recession. That every family is harboring someone still not back at work. That someone is paying rent for their brother-in-law. And then a guy comes on the stage and says, "I'm your guy who will blow the whole thing up."[65]

Blue-collar Democrats, in particular, like Trump's position on the economy: "In terms of his message, it is really resonating. Particularly if you are talking [about] union people, he is speaking our language."[66] Trump has become the first Republican who, since Ronald Reagan's win in 1980, has been able to foster a strong appeal among union workers. They believe that he is going to fight for them.

Providing Assurance

Similarly, cognitive dissonance[67] creates discomfort when people see a conflict between their divergent views or between their views and their behavior. People are highly motivated to maintain consistency in their views and in order to preserve them, they perform irrational and even maladaptive behavior. To reduce cognitive dissonance and restore harmony between their attitudes and beliefs, people can choose several strategies. One approach is to change their self-perception, to recognize bad behavior, and to accept new negative information about themselves. People typically avoid this tactic, however. They also can change or eliminate the behavior causing cognitive dissonance. For example, people can stop smoking because of the negative effects on their health. A second strategy is to change their perception about the situation, thus justifying their behavior or creating new information about it. People who smoke disregard warnings about the lethal effects of the habit and may consider medical research unconvincing. A third strategy is to reduce the importance of the belief or change it drastically. People can create the new belief that for them, life with the pleasure of smoking is more important than a longer but less pleasurable life without it. Generally, they prefer to maintain their positive self-image and consistent beliefs and, thus, typically change their view depending on the situation. "I was late not because I am not well organized, but because traffic was unpredictable." "We failed this project not because we did not have the required proficiencies, but because the existing information was inconsistent."

Many Trump supporters who have a negative perception of immigrants, Muslims, African Americans, or other groups do not want to accept that their views may be biased or even bigoted in some cases. They feel comfort when Trump expresses similar opinions publicly: it helps them to justify their positions. Trump has created a space in which negative perceptions of others can be expressed openly. His supporters do not see his remarks on various issues as exclusionary or discriminatory. As one supporter stated, "Some people call his immigration [proposals] racist, blah, blah, blah. There's nothing racist about saying there shouldn't be illegal immigrants here. They're illegal immigrants for a reason."[68] Another supporter echoed this sentiment, stating, "None of his policies are racist."[69] Justifying his comments about women's bodies, one female supporter noted,

> He has a wife and daughter, so I believe that somewhere down the line, he understands the needs of a woman. And though he might have said those remarks, I don't think he really meant them in, like, a harmful way or anything like that.[70]

Discussing support for Trump by the former KKK leader, David Duke, which Trump did not disavow, one supporter stated,

> Honestly, people are going to talk no matter what and try their best to bring him down because they don't like what he stands for now and the way he puts his spin on things. So no, it doesn't really bother me. But I feel like now he's going to become a better person, he's really trying to make America great again, and that's what I believe.[71]

This support for Trump is also based on the confirmation bias.[72] People tend to seek out information that is in line with previously held beliefs. They also lend more weight to informational input that supports their beliefs, while discarding contradictory information.[73] The confirmation bias is related to a common human desire to be right and to avoid embarrassment brought about by recanting on a previously held belief. Confirmation bias can also ensure that entrenched religious, ideological, and ethical beliefs are not challenged, therefore, making believers feel more confident.

Trump has echoed the views of his supporters through the ways in which he addresses issues of immigration, refugees, and the feeling of economic deprivation among his voters. They actively look for information verifying their ideas and feel satisfied with Trump's positions. Trump supporters find confirmation for their existing biases and prejudices in his speeches, which serve to increase their connection to him. Moreover, the negative nicknames Trump has created for his opponents, like "Crooked Hillary" and "Lying Ted," have stuck because they confirm already established beliefs among his supporters. As one supporter noted, "What Trump is saying is the truth because he can afford to say it. A lot of the other candidates don't feel like they can afford to say it, because they'd bite the hand that feeds."[74] Another supporter similarly stated, "I'm for Trump because he talks about Muslims the way we talk about Muslims."[75] Because Trump confirms their existing views, many supporters believe he "sees what's going on in the country"[76] and "tells it like it is."[77]

Trump has continually championed ideas that are in line with his supporters' views on many issues, which helps to justify their theories about the world and their suspicions. Sixty-five percent of Trump's supporters think President Obama is, like his Kenyan father, a Muslim and 59 percent think President Obama was not born in the U.S.[78] This latter statistic strongly resonates with Trump's "birther" movement, which questioned President Obama's U.S. citizenship.

Pertinently, Trump supporters have also been susceptible to accepting new attitudes that go beyond their established perceptions and beliefs: "I support him because he has taken everything that we've learned about American politics or everything that we have been taught, and he has molded it into this giant middle finger that's pointed toward the establishment."[79] Moreover, they start to see themselves as agents of his will, carrying out his wishes as if their own, and they lay all responsibility for their actions with Trump.[80]

In order to understand how such behavior is justifiable, in the next chapter, we will explore the changes that have taken root regarding people's moral outlook.

Notes

1. Parsons, Talcott. *Essays in Sociological Theory.* Glencoe, Ill: Free Press, 1954: 126, accessed June 1, 2016, http://archive.org/details/sociologicaltheo00pars.

2. Snow, David A., and Robert D. Benford. "Ideology, Frame Resonance, and Participant Mobilization," in *International Social Movement Research: From Structure to Action*, ed. Bert Klandermans, H Kriesi, and Sidney G Tarrow. Greenwich, CO: JAI Press, 1988: 197–217.
3. Erving, Goffman. *Frame Analysis: An Essay on the Organization of Experience.* Harper & Row, 1974.
4. Tilly, Charles. *Regimes and Repertoires*. Chicago: University of Chicago Press, 2006; Tilly, Charles. *The Politics of Collective Violence*. Cambridge: Cambridge University Press, 2003.
5. Fox, Lauren. "Trump Calls Rubio 'Little Marco' as GOP Debate Goes Off the Rails," *TalkingPointsMemo*, March 3, 2016, accessed June 3, 2016, http://talking pointsmemo.com/livewire/trump-belittles-rubio-little-marco
6. Dicker, Rachel. "Donald Trump's #LittleMarco Is the Internet's New Favorite Thing," *US News*, March 4, 2016, accessed May 17, 2016, http://www.usnews. com/news/articles/2016–03–04/donald-trump-called-marco-rubio-little-marco-at-the-gop-debate-and-twitter-went-crazy
7. Lazzaro, Sage. "11 Hilarious 'Little Marco' Memes Mocking Rubio's Florida Loss," *Observer*, March 16, 2016, accessed June 1, 2016, http://observer. com/2016/03/11-hilarious-little-marco-memes-mocking-rubios-florida-loss/
8. Hensch, Mark. "Trump Swaggers through Super Tuesday Rally," *The Hill*, March 1, 2016, accessed May 29, 2016, http://thehill.com/blogs/ballot-box/ presidential-races/271298-trump-swaggers-way-through-ohio-rally-on-super-tuesday
9. Kamisar, Ben. "Trump Digs at Cruz, Calling Him 'Lying Ted,'" *The Hill*, March 3, 2016, accessed June 2, 2016, http://thehill.com/blogs/ballot-box/ presidential-races/271746-trump-digs-at-cruz-calling-him-lying-ted
10. Gurciullo, Brianna. "Trump Revives 'Lyin' Ted' Attack on Cruz," *Politico*, April 20, 2016, accessed, June 2, 2016, http://www.politico.com/blogs/2016-gop-primary-live-updates-and-results/2016/04/trump-ted-cruz-lying-222226#ixzz49aRG5oML
11. Hoft, Jim. "TRUMP Blasts Crooked Hillary On Her Dangerous Refugee Plan That Only 4% of Women Support," *The Gateway Pundit*, May 24, 2016, accessed May 30, 2016, http://www.thegatewaypundit.com/2016/05/ wow-protesters-call-ted-cruz-lyin-ted-face-video/
12. Voorhees, Josh. "John Boehner Compares Ted Cruz to Satan, Says He Wouldn't Vote for Him in November," *Slate*, April 28, 2016, accessed June 2, 2016, http:// www.slate.com/blogs/the_slatest/2016/04/28/john_boehner_reportedly_called_ ted_cruz_lucifer_in_the_flesh.html
13. Biddle, Sam. "Ted Cruz, We've Caught You in a Lie," *Gawker*, April 28, 2016, accessed June 2, 2016, http://gawker.com/ted-cruz-weve-caught-you-in-a-lie-1773630713
14. Kreutz, Liz. "Hillary Clinton Says: 'I Really Could Care Less' about Donald Trump Calling Her 'Crooked Hillary,'" *Yahoo*, April 17, 2016, accessed May 30, 2016, https://gma.yahoo.com/hillary-clinton-says-really-could-care-less-donald-142713928.html
15. Hains, Tim. "Trump Pivots to Hillary: "She's Always Been a Crooked Person," *RealClear Politics*, April 24, 2016, accessed May 30, 2016, http://www.real clearpolitics.com/video/2016/04/24/donald_trump_raises_whitewater_clinton_ foundation_corruption_shes_always_been_a_crooked_person.html
16. Trump, Donald J. "How can Crooked Hillary say she cares about women when she is silent on radical Islam, which horribly oppresses women?" *Twitter*, May 22,

2016, accessed May 29, 2016, https://mobile.twitter.com/realDonaldTrump/status/734468142303305728

17. Howerton, Jason. "Trump Says If 'Crooked Hillary' Really Wants to 'Get Rid of' Guns, She Should Do This First," *The Blaze*, May 22, 2016, accessed May 30, 2016, http://www.theblaze.com/stories/2016/05/22/trump-says-if-crooked-hillary-really-wants-to-get-rid-of-guns-she-should-do-this-first/

18. Hahn, Julia. "Trump: Hillary Can't Say She Cares about Women while Importing Radical Refugees to America," *Reuters*, May 23, 2016, accessed May 30, 2016, http://www.breitbart.com/2016-presidential-race/2016/05/23/trump-hillary-cant-say-cares-women-importing-radical-refugees-america/

19. Hoft, Jim. "TRUMP Blasts Crooked Hillary on Her Dangerous Refugee Plan That Only 4% of Women Support," *The Gateway Pundit*, May 24, 2016, accessed May 30, 2016, http://www.thegatewaypundit.com/2016/05/trump-blasts-crooked-hillary-dangerous-refugee-plan-4-women-support/

20. Graham, David A. "Why Trump Might Regret Playing 'The Women Card' Against Clinton," *The Atlantic*, April 27, 2016, accessed May 30, 2016, http://www.theatlantic.com/politics/archive/2016/04/trump-hillary-clinton-woman-card/480129/

21. Trump, "How Can Crooked Hillary Say She Cares about Women."

22. Kahn, Chris. "Exclusive: Top Reason Americans Will Vote for Trump: 'To Stop Clinton'—Poll," *Reuters*, May 9, 2016, accessed May 26, 2016, http://www.reuters.com/article/us-usa-election-anti-vote-idUSKCN0XX06E

23. Berger, C. R., and Bradac, J. J. *Language and Social Knowledge: Uncertainty in Interpersonal Relations*. London: Arnold, 1982.

24. Ladouceur, R., Talbot, F., and M. J. Duglas, "Behavioral expressions of intolerance of uncertainty in worry." *Behav Modif* 21, no. 3 (July 1997): 355–371.

25. CNN Staff. "Transcript of Republican Debate in Miami, Full Text," *CNN*, March 15, 2016, accessed May 30, 2016, http://www.cnn.com/2016/03/10/politics/republican-debate-transcript-full-text/

26. Itkowitz, Colby. " 'Little Marco,' 'Lyin' Ted,' 'Crooked Hillary:' How Donald Trump makes Name Calling Stick," *The Washington Post*, April 20, 2016, accessed May 29, 2016, https://www.washingtonpost.com/news/inspired-life/wp/2016/04/20/little-marco-lying-ted-crooked-hillary-donald-trumps-winning-strategy-nouns/

27. CNN Staff. "Transcript of Republican debate in Miami."

28. Ibid.

29. Lee, M. J., and Dan Merica. "Clinton Looks to Pop Trump's Populist Appeal," *CNN*, May 25, 2016, accessed May 27, 2016, http://www.cnn.com/2016/05/24/politics/hillary-clinton-donald-trump-populist-housing-crisis/

30. Reich, Robert. "Why Trump Might Win," *RealClear Politics*, May 24, 2016, accessed May 29, 2016, http://www.realclearpolitics.com/articles/2016/05/24/why_trump_might_win_130653.html

31. Holmes, Jamie. *Nonsense: The Power of Not Knowing*. Crown Publishing, 2015.

32. Neuberg, Steven L., Judice, T. Nicole., West, Stephen G. "What the need for closure scale measures and what it does not: Toward differentiating among related epistemic motives." *Journal of Personality and Social Psychology*, 72, no. 6, (1997): 1396–1412.

33. Long, Heather, and Patrick Gillpesie. "Why Americans Are so Angry in 2016," *CNN Money*, March 9, 2016, accessed May 1, 2016, http://money.cnn.com/2016/03/09/news/economy/donald-trump-bernie-sanders-angry-america/?version=meter+at+6&module=meter-Links&pgtype=article&contentId=&mediaId=&referrer=&priority=true&action=click&contentCollection=meter-links-click

34. Ibid.
35. Huffinton Post Staff. "Poll Chart: US Right Direction Wrong Track," *Huffpost Pollster*, continually updated, accessed May 5, 2016, "http://elections.huffington post.com/pollster/us-right-direction-wrong-track?version=meter+at+6&module= meter-Links&pgtype=article&contentId=&mediaId=&referrer=&priority=true& action=click&contentCollection=meter-links-click
36. Long,and Gillpesie. "Why Americans Are So Angry in 2016."
37. Nichols, John. "President Donald J. Trump—It Could Happen." *The Nation*, February 23, 2016, accessed March 28, 2016, http://www.thenation.com/article/ why-donald-trumps-populism-is-dangerous/
38. Ibid.
39. Asch, S.E. "Forming impressions of personality." *Journal of Abnormal and Social Psychology*, 41, (1946): 258–290.
40. Reich, Robert. "Why Trump Might Win." *RealClear Politics*, May 24, 2016, accessed May 29, 2016, http://www.realclearpolitics.com/articles/2016/05/24/ why_trump_might_win_130653.html
41. Nyhan, Brendan. "Why Republicans Are Suddenly Talking About Economic Inequality," *New York Times*, February 13, 2016, accessed March 30, 2016, http://www.nytimes.com/2015/02/14/upshot/why-republicans-are-suddenly-talking-about-economic-inequality.html?abt=0002&abg=1&_r=0
42. Sides, John and Michael Tesler. "How Political Science Helps Explain the Rise of Trump: Most Voters Aren't Ideological," *The Washington Post*, March 2, 2016, accessed March 27, 2016 https://www.washingtonpost.com/news/monkey-cage/ wp/2016/03/02/how-political-science-helps-explain-the-rise-of-trump-most-voters-arent-ideologues/
43. Ibid.
44. Frum, "The Great Republican Revolt."
45. Sides, John. "Republican Primary Voters Embrace Government. No, Really," *The Monkey Cage*, March 22, 2012, accessed May 27, 2016, http://themonkeycage. org/2012/03/republican-primary-voters-embrace-government-no-really/
46. Armitage, C.J., and Comer, M. "The effects of ambivalence on attitude stability and pliability, prediction of behavior, and information processing." *Personality and Social Psychology Bulletin*, 26, (2000): 1432–1443.
47. Cillizza, Chris. "Donald Trump Did a CNN Townhall Last Night. And It Was a Classic." *The Washington Post*, March 30, 2016, accessed May 28, 2016, https://www.washingtonpost.com/news/the-fix/wp/2016/03/30/donald-trump-did-a-cnn-townhall-last-night-and-it-was-a-classic/
48. Ibid.
49. Lehmann, Chris. "Donald Trump and the Long Tradition of American Populism," *Newsweek*, August 22, 2015, accessed April 2, 2016, http://www.newsweek. com/donald-trump-populism-365052
50. The Wall Street Journal Staff. "Donald Trump Transcript: 'Our Country Needs a Truly Great Leader,'" *The Wall Street Journal*, June 16, 2016, accessed June 20, 2016, http://blogs.wsj.com/washwire/2015/06/16/ donald-trump-transcript-our-country-needs-a-truly-great-leader/
51. CNN Staff. "Transcript of Republican Debate in Miami, Full Text," *CNN*, March 15, 2016, accessed May 29, 2016, http://www.cnn.com/2016/03/10/ politics/republican-debate-transcript-full-text/
52. Chalt, Jonathan. "Trump vs. Everybody Is the New McCain vs. Bush," *New Yorker: News & Politics*, September 2, 2015, accessed May 27, 2016, http://nymag.

com/daily/intelligencer/2015/09/trump-vs-everybody-is-the-new-mccain-vs-bush.html

53. Sides, John, and Michael Tesler. "How Political Science Helps Explain the Rise of Trump: Most Voters Aren't Ideological," *The Washington Post*, March 2, 2016, accessed April 3, 2016, https://www.washingtonpost.com/news/monkey-cage/wp/2016/03/02/how-political-science-helps-explain-the-rise-of-trump-most-voters-arent-ideologues/

54. Drutman, Lee. "What Donald Trump Gets about the Electorate," *Vox*, August 18, 2015, accessed April 2, 2016, http://www.vox.com/2015/8/18/9172653/trump-populism-immigration

55. Lerner, Will. "Donald Trump Defends Andrew Jackson during Town Hall on 'Today,'" *Yahoo*, April 21, 2016, accessed May 1, 2016, https://www.yahoo.com/news/donald-trump-defends-andrew-jackson-during-town-195147314.html?nhp=1

56. Cillizza, Chris. "Donald Trump did a CNN Townhall Last Night. And It was a Classic," *The Washington Post*, March 30, 2016, accessed May 20, 2016, https://www.washingtonpost.com/news/the-fix/wp/2016/03/30/donald-trump-did-a-cnn-townhall-last-night-and-it-was-a-classic/

57. Schreckinger, Ben. "Donald Trump: 'This is a Movement,'" *Politico*, August 29, 2015, accessed April 4, 2016, http://www.politico.com/story/2015/08/donald-trump-2016-movement-213160#ixzz4AuDO5PjQ

58. Kaczynski, Andrew and Nathan McDermott. "In 2002, Donald Trump Said He Supported Invading Iraq," *BuzzFeed News*, February 18, 2016, accessed May 26, 2016, https://www.buzzfeed.com/andrewkaczynski/in-2002-donald-trump-said-he-supported-invading-iraq-on-the?utm_term=.pbzw3jApDE#.baeEdYVRPD

59. Trump, Donald J. "Donald Trump: How I'd Run the Country (Better)," *Esquire*, August 18, 2016, accessed June 1, 2016, http://www.esquire.com/news-politics/interviews/a37230/donald-trump-esquire-cover-story-august-2004/

60. April 4, 2016 issue of *Time*.

61. Ferris, Sarah. "Poll: 20% of Dems Would Defect for Trump," *The Hill*, January 9, 2016, accessed May 25, 2016, http://thehill.com/homenews/campaign/265330-some-dems-would-defect-for-trump-poll-shows

62. Crowley, Monica. "How Donald Trump Is Drawing in Democrats," *The Washington Times*, May 18, 2016, accessed May 19, 2016, http://www.washingtontimes.com/news/2016/may/18/monica-crowley-how-donald-trump-is-drawing-in-demo/

63. Trump, Donald J. *America We Deserve*.

64. Jamieson, Dave. "Donald Trump Is Killing It with White, Working-Class Voters In the Rust Belt," *The Huffington Post*, January 28, 2016, accessed April 9, 2016, http://www.huffingtonpost.com/entry/donald-trump-working-class-voters_us_56aa44d0e4b0d82286d51ffa

65. Stein, Sam and Dave Jamieson. "Donald Trump's Working-Class Appeal Is Starting to Freak Out Labor Unions," *The Huffington Post*, March 17, 2016, accessed April 9, 2016, http://www.huffingtonpost.com/entry/donald-trump-working-class-unions_us_56ead51fe4b03a640a69c58d

66. Ibid.

67. Festinger, L. *A Theory of Cognitive Dissonance*. Stanford, CA: Stanford University Press, 1957.

68. Gupta, Prachi. "Female College Students Explain Why They Support Donald Trump," *Cosmopolitan*, March 4, 2016, accessed May 19, 2016, http://www.cosmopolitan.com/politics/news/a54718/college-students-donald-trump-supporters/

69. Ibid.
70. Ibid.
71. Ibid.
72. Weiner, B. *An Attributional Theory of Motivation and Emotion.* New York: Springer-Verlag, 1986.
73. Nickerson, Raymond S. "Confirmation Bias: A Ubiquitous Phenomenon in Many Guises." *Review of General Psychology*, 2, no. 2 (1988): 175–220, accessed May 19, 2016, http://psy2.ucsd.edu/~mckenzie/nickersonConfirmationBias.pdf
74. Wofford, Ben. "Meet the Liberals Who Think Trump's Good for Democracy," *Politico Magazine*, August 25, 2015, accessed April 7, 2016, http://www.politico.com/magazine/story/2015/08/meet-the-liberals-who-love-trump-121733#ixzz48vSVaQtb
75. February 22, 2016 issue of *Time*.
76. Taylor, "Why Trump Is Here to Stay."
77. Schreckinger, Ben. "Trump, Alabama and the Ghost of George Wallace," *Politico*, August 21, 2015, accessed May 1, 2016, http://www.politico.com/story/2015/08/donald-trump-2016-mobile-alabama-rally-ghost-george-wallace-121627#ixzz3jkOWPAR1
78. Public Leadership Institute. "New Poll Illustrates Confirmation Bias, Trump Less Popular than Lice," *Public Leadership Institute*, May 10, 2016, accessed May 19*, 2016*, http://www.publicleadershipinstitute.org/new_poll_illustrates_confirmation_bias_trump_less_popular_than_lice
79. Gupta, Prachi. "Female College Students Explain Why They Support Donald Trump," *Cosmopolitan*, March 4, 2016, accessed May 16, 2016, http://www.cosmopolitan.com/politics/news/a54718/college-students-donald-trump-supporters/
80. Milgram, Stanley. *Obedience to Authority: An Experimental View.* Harpercollins, 1974.

6 The Good, the Bad, and the Ugly

Similarly to the need for cognitive certainty, people prefer to face clear and simple moral judgments. Those who approach moral questions in a simple manner, reducing moral decision making to a strict binary between two opposing options, are often perceived as displaying strength, whereas approaches to moral questions that consider multiple views are perceived as a sign of weakness, and a compromise is viewed as a mark of capitulation. Trump provides his supporters with a clear and distinct moral system, free of moral dilemmas and "political correctness." Trump achieves this by drawing upon dualistic morality, specific collective axiology, and the imperial stage of ethics.

People often see the world in terms of "good" and bad." This undeveloped and often crude way of viewing the world emphasizes dualities that replicate an essentialist contrast between the sacred and the profane.[1] These dualities always have a positive and a negative value[2] and form our perception of the world, which is premised on opposites.[3] The simple logic behind such dualities and the way in which they may be quickly recalled make them easy for people to use, especially if they are supporting a leader who utilizes them.[4] These dualities help create and maintain a straightforward understanding of society and constantly reproduce the perception of "us" versus "them."[5]

Dual political systems, such as the one existing in the U.S., also contribute to the development of dualities and binary oppositions. In the last fifteen years, politics has become more central to Americans' self-identity. In the U.S., the dual opposition between Republicans and Democrats is now greater than gender, age, race, or class divisions.[6] Over the last twenty-five years, the average gap in values and positions between Democrats and Republicans has nearly doubled. The most significant increase in this gap occurred during the presidencies of George W. Bush and Barack Obama. This is partly because the negative views held among Democrats of George W. Bush were similar in their negativity to the opinions among Republicans today toward Barak Obama.[7] Moreover, the polarization of racial attitudes has significantly increased since the election of President Obama, creating a "most-racial" political era.[8]

Another explanation for the growing ideological gap between the Republican and Democratic parties is a structural problem: the widening gap between rich and poor. "The states that have the highest levels of inequality, or the fastest growth in equality, have also tended to see the most political polarization."[9] Similarly, the increase in cultural diversity in the U.S. has contributed to a heightened degree of political polarization.

Whereas the number of independents has recently increased, both conservatives and liberals have become more ideologically homogeneous. Positions within political parties have also changed: Republicans are more united around minimizing the role of government and reducing the regulatory overreach by environmentalism. Democrats have become more socially liberal and secular.[10] The percentage of Democrats who express liberal views on most issues has nearly doubled from just 30 percent in 1994 to 56 percent in 2014. Similarly, while in 1994, 13 percent of Republicans were consistently conservative, in 2014, their numbers almost doubled to 20 percent.[11] Political institutions have also become more sharply divided: "Congress is now more polarized than at any time since the end of Reconstruction."[12]

The growing difference between the parties is reflected in their approaches to many issues. For example, the gap between the parties view on racial equality has doubled since 1987: 52 percent of Democrats are supportive of efforts to improve racial equality, whereas only 12 percent of Republicans agree with this view.[13] While in 1992, only 30 percent of Democrats thought the Confederate flag symbolized racism, in 2015, this percentage doubled, creating a 44 percent gap between Democrats and Republicans.[14] Another poll showed Democrats were five times more likely than Republicans to see the flag as a primarily racist symbol.[15] Opinion is also divided over whether the U.S. should increase foreign aid to developing countries: 62 percent of Democrats support this idea, whereas only 32 percent of Republicans agree.[16]

Democrats and Republicans not only are divided by different views, but they also harbor a growing hostility toward members of the opposition party, which is impacting the everyday life of people in the U.S. Forty-three percent of Republicans have a highly negative opinion of the Democratic Party, whereas 38 percent of Democrats feel very unfavorably toward the GOP.[17] In comparison with 1960, Democrats and Republicans were nearly 50 percent more likely to attribute negative features to opponents in 2010.[18] People willingly discriminate against the members of the opposite party.[19] In 1960, only 5 percent of Americans said they would be upset if their child married a supporter of a different party. In 2010, a third of Democrats and half of Republicans said that they would be.[20]

The divide in values has also been connected to education levels. Educated young people have become more liberal on social issues, which includes an acceptance of different gender identities and LGBTQ rights, support for same-sex marriage, and a tolerance of diversity and more secular values. People from more traditionalist backgrounds feel threatened by this change in values and see themselves as marginalized and left behind within their own country.[21] These groups believe that "political correctness" is changing the country for the worse.

This political polarization has contributed significantly to the strong support enjoyed by Trump in two ways. First, it draws people toward him who might disagree with him but hold staunchly negative opinions of Clinton and are becoming more fearful of the opposing party. In 2014, more than a quarter of Democrats and more than a third of Republicans viewed the other party as "a threat to the nation's well-being."[22] Sixty-six percent of conservatives perceive Democratic policies as a threat to the country and 50 percent of liberals believe Republican policies are a threat.[23] As opinion polls have shown, almost half of all voters support either Clinton or Trump because they do not want the other party and its respective candidate to win.[24]

About 47 percent of Trump supporters said they would vote for him because they did not want Clinton to win. Only 43 percent of Trump's supporters like his political positions and only 6 percent like him personally. As one Trump supporter stated, "If I had to pick one of those, I'd vote for Trump." Another supporter similarly stated, "What choice do I have? I really don't trust Hillary Clinton." Yet another explains her choice to support Trump over Clinton: "Hillary Clinton is not being held accountable. The fact that she's going to be the Democratic nominee having this [e-mail scandal] hanging over her head, I just can't understand that."[25]

The dislike toward Clinton has even served to motivate people to vote for Trump who are traditionally Democratic voters. Around 20 percent of Sanders supporters stated they would vote for Trump because they detested Clinton or see Trump as a better candidate in comparison to Clinton.[26] As one Democratic voter wrote,

> I don't want to vote for Trump. I want to vote for Bernie. But I have reached the point where I feel like voting for Trump against Clinton would be doing my patriotic duty. . .. If the only way to escape a trap is to gnaw off my leg, I'd like to think I'd have the guts to do it.[27]

Yves Smith, a writer for *Politico* noted,

> To be sure, not all of my Sanders-supporting readers would vote for Trump. But only a minority would ever vote for Clinton . . . Some of them also have very reasoned arguments for Trump. Hillary is a known evil. Trump is unknown. They'd rather bet on the unknown.[28]

Eighty percent of Republican voters believe the leaders of the party should unite and support Donald J. Trump.²⁹ As one Republican voter stated,

> The reason I would support him is because the alternative is less favorable, in my opinion. And I think Republican leaders should support him for the same reason I am supporting him. The alternative is not palatable to those of us who hold conservative views.³⁰

Speaker of the House, Paul Ryan, endorsed Trump after a long period of disagreement and criticism:

> As I said from the start, my goal has been to unite the party so we can win in the fall. And if we're going to unite, it has to be over ideas. It's no secret that he and I have our differences. . ... But the reality is, on the issues that make up our agenda, we have more common ground than disagreement.³¹

He also stressed that preventing Clinton from becoming president was the main aim of the party: "A Clinton White House would mean four more years of liberal cronyism and a government more out for itself than the people it serves. Quite simply, she represents all that our agenda aims to fix."³² Former Speaker of the House, Newt Gingrich, supported this position: "Speaker Paul Ryan showed real leadership in patiently working through key issues and then endorsing Trump. The right way to do it."³³ Many former presidential rivals of Trump have also joined him, including Marco Rubio, Bobby Jindal, and Scott Walker.

The National Rifle Association's endorsement of Trump is also rooted in their opposition to Clinton. Getting the support of the NRA was crucial for Trump. Trump's relationship with the association has not always been harmonious. In 2000, in his *The America We Deserve*, Trump stated,

> I generally oppose gun control, but I support the ban on assault weapons and I also support a slightly longer waiting period to purchase a gun. With today's Internet technology we should be able to tell within seventy-two hours if a potential gun owner has a record.³⁴

Fifteen years later, in *Crippled America: How to Make America Great Again*, he reversed his position:

> The Supreme Court has made it clear that the Government simply has no business, and in fact, no rights to dictate to gun owners what types of firearm the law-abiding Americans are allowed to own. Gun owners should be allowed to purchase the best type of weapon for their needs.³⁵

As a presidential candidate, Trump has continually shown his support for the NRA but has also capitalized on the fear of Clinton as president in order to garner support. In his speech to the NRA, Trump built upon this anti-Clinton sentiment, which proved highly effective in terms of gaining supporters:

> The Second Amendment is under a threat like never before. Crooked Hillary Clinton is the most anti-gun . . . candidate ever to run for office. And, as I said before, she wants to abolish the Second Amendment. She wants to take your guns away. She wants to abolish it.[36]

This anti-Clinton approach worked well to draw NRA members to the Trump camp. As NRA chief Wayne LaPierre noted, "If she could, Hillary would ban every gun, destroy every magazine, run an entire national security industry right into the ground and put your name on a government registration list."[37] Chris Cox, the executive director of the NRA's Institute for Legislative Action, stressed that united support for Trump was a necessary step in preventing Clinton from imposing her policies: "Now is the time to unite. If your preferred candidate dropped out of the race, it's time to get over it."[38]

Second, Trump has sought to build on a point of moral antagonism that currently exists in American society by promoting simpler, dualistic views. He employs dualities his supporters then use to define what is right and what is wrong, what is good and what is bad, what is sacred and what is profane. He has emphasized threats to national prosperity and security and has clearly defined internal and external enemies and allies. Using these moral dualities, Trump is able to justify changes to existing societal norms and to create sound justifications for policies of inclusion and exclusion.

Tribal dualities of exclusion and fearful bias are primitive in their nature and thus are mostly stereotypical and extremely powerful. As a result, they become highly influential among people who adopt them easily. This, in turn, has the effect of redefining their existing moral code. Particular tribal dualities can easily overshadow established civic ethics of inclusion and integrity.[39] These codes of exclusion still prevail in societies across the globe and are based on social categories such as gender, kinship, ethnicity, religion or race.[40] They define social boundaries as rigid and proscribe certain ethnic, racial, or national groups from joining the dominant group because of "a threat of pollution."[41] People justify the exclusion of particular groups based on stories regarding their shared past, implicit and explicit rules, traditions, and social routines.

This definition of dualistic morality allows Trump to employ to his advantage negative interracial perceptions, fears of terrorism, and threats to jobs. Trump has sought to define exclusive criteria for American citizenship, which consists of barring certain groups, such as illegal Mexican immigrants and Muslims, from the possibility of obtaining it. As Roger Stone, a Republican consultant stated, nobody does tribal warfare better than Trump: "It's us-against-them politics. You define yourself by who your enemies are."[42] Further, Trump divides the world into winners and losers, evil and good, laborers and parasites. And he provides his supporters with assurances that they are on the right side. "Donald Trump has created the us-versus-them story, the winner-versus-loser story. And people always want to be [aligned] with the winner."[43]

Trump's dual framing of these moral codes makes them easily adopted by his supporters. Trump supporters see him as authentic because he uses and further develops moral dualities that are deeply incorporated in values and perceptions of particular groups as a result of historical interactions with the Other. The leadership of the group Women Vote Trump stated, "We know he's not perfect. But he's genuine, and that's a breath of fresh air. He will keep my family safe from outside threats and illegal immigration."[44] Trump has echoed the perceptions of his supporters by identifying "good" and "bad" groups and specifying their rightful positions within society. As one of his supporters stated, "I love Donald Trump because he's totally politically incorrect. He's gone after every group."[45] Another supporter echoed this sentiment by noting, "He's saying the things no one else says."[46]

Already deeply frustrated by the perception of an increasing threat of terrorism, there was an outcry among segments of the American public following the largest mass killing in American history, which took place in a popular gay nightclub in Orlando in June 2016 and left forty-nine people dead and fifty-three wounded. However, the reaction of people differed. There was an outpouring of support for and solidarity with the LGBTQ community on the one hand and strong anti-Muslim sentiments on the other. President Obama framed the shooting as "an act of terror and an act of hate" and called for solidarity.[47] He avoided labeling the attack as the result of "Islamic extremism" but rather concentrated on the specifics of the shooting as a singular act of terror. Many people felt he did not demonstrate the required leadership America needed at that moment and did not highlight the actual roots of the problem.[48] Republicans immediately emphasized his weakness on national security and the futility of the current administration's approach to the threat of ISIS.[49]

Trump's reaction to the Orlando shooting reinforced his preferred moral positioning of duality between "vicious Muslims" and a "victimized America." Trump capitalized on this opportunity to confirm his stance on the threat of Islam and Islamic terrorism, in addition to the moral duality between good and evil. In his first tweet after the shooting, Trump wrote, "Appreciate the congrats for being right on radical Islamic terrorism, I don't want congrats, I want toughness & vigilance. We must be smart!"[50] He immediately blamed President Obama for being unable to defend the U.S. In a Fox News interview on the morning after the attack, Trump made remarks suggesting the president was possibly sympathetic to Islamic terrorists:

> Look, we're led by a man that either is not tough, not smart, or he's got something else in mind. And the something else in mind—you know, people can't believe it. People cannot, they cannot believe that President Obama is acting the way he acts and can't even mention the words "radical Islamic terrorism." There's something going on. It's inconceivable. There's something going on.[51]

Trump stated all Muslim immigrants present a potential threat to American society and reiterated his proposition to ban migrants from parts of the world with "a proven history of terrorism" against the U.S. or its allies. He blamed American Muslims in general for failing to "turn in the people who they know are bad," including the shooters in Orlando and San Bernardino. "They didn't turn them in and we had death and destruction."[52] "The Muslims have to work with us," Trump said. "They know what is going on."[53]

Trump also blamed the current administration's immigration policy, stating, it [the government] created an "immigration system, which does not permit us to know who we let into our country." Trump went further, noting, "The bottom line is that the only reason the killer was in America in the first place was because we allowed his family to come here."[54] Once again, Trump reiterated his call to ban Muslims from entering the U.S., which he initially made in the wake of the San Bernardino shooting in December 2015. Describing the ban as a restriction for countries involved in terrorist actions, Trump stated,

> Although the pause is temporary, we must find out what is going on. We have to do it. It will be lifted, this ban, when as a nation we're in a position to properly and perfectly screen these people coming into our country. They're pouring in and we don't know what we're doing.[55]

He has said such vigilance is a necessary measure and that the U.S. "can't afford to be politically correct."[56]

Trump has, thus, not only represented but also shaped values that intensify group differences. [57] He has provided his supporters with a particular view of the social problems facing the U.S., has sought to shape their perceptions pertaining to a necessary course of action, and has, lastly, created a basis for evaluating members of different groups. His descriptions of Muslims and Americans through the use of categories of right/wrong, good/bad, and virtuous/vicious justify specific obligations, expectations, requirements, demands, and rights of these groups. He has sought to redefine the boundaries of American citizenship and established criteria for inclusion and exclusion in the nation. Trump has created a high level of generality[58] by describing Muslims in the U.S. and abroad as one singular group. He defines Muslims as a unitary, homogeneous group that demonstrates fixed patterns of dangerous behaviors and that is committed to rigid radical beliefs and values. This unbalanced morality[59] has led to a more prominent and open perception of Muslims as an evil and vicious group, which has resulted in making the virtues of Americans and vices of Muslims as somehow fixed in a timeless social order.[60]

Democrats immediately sought to label Trump's call to ban Muslims as an absurd proposal that would create an exclusive America. President Barack Obama called Trump's ideas a "dangerous" mind-set.[61] Many Republicans also expressed criticism of his approach. Speaker of the House, Paul Ryan, expressed his opposition to such a ban on Muslim immigration, stating such a religiously based policy was alien to the U.S. and inconsistent with the principles of Republicans: "This is a war with radical Islam. It is not a war with Islam."[62]

Some legal scholars and politicians have, however, supported Trump, stressing that such a policy could be necessary to defend America's security. They cited similar policies in U.S. history, reminding the public, for instance, that Democratic president Jimmy Carter barred Iranian nationals from entering the U.S. during the 1979 Iran hostage crisis.[63] Trump has also received wide support from voters. Exit polls during the Republican primaries showed a large majority of voters would approve a temporary ban on Muslims entering the country, from 63 percent in Virginia to 78 percent in Alabama.[64] Among the population of the U.S., 50 percent of voters support a temporary halt on Muslim entry into the country.[65] That includes 71 percent of Republican voters and 34 percent of Democratic voters.[66] As one voter stated, "He is a rough talker, but it's not a big deal. Everybody seems so thin-skinned. I don't believe we can continue to go in the direction we're going. We've got to change our direction."[67]

In response to the Orlando shooting, Trump also drew a line between "us" and "them," fusing terrorists and the current Democratic leadership together to form one group comprising dangerous agents. Trump placed complete responsibility for the attack on President Obama, noting that his policies were dangerous for the country: "I said this was going to happen—and it is only going to get worse." [68] Trump also stated that he will change President Obama's policies immediately: "If I get in (the White House), it's going to change, and it's going to change quickly. We're going from total incompetence to just the opposite, believe me."[69] Finally, he warned against a Clinton presidency by underlining that it would bring "hundreds of thousands" more Middle Eastern migrants who may pose a threat to U.S. security. "And we

will have no way to screen them, pay for them, or prevent the second generation from radicalizing."[70] Trump also added that "Hillary Clinton can never
claim to be a friend of the gay community," as long as she supports immigration from nations that oppress homosexuality.[71]

On the other hand, Trump showed his support and sympathy for the rest of
the country. First, he highlighted his influence over the NRA, noting that he
would be discussing a deal with them that would contribute to the safety of
the American public and, at the same time, preserve the Second Amendment.

> I will be meeting with the NRA—which has given me their earliest
> endorsement in a presidential race—to discuss how to ensure Ameri-
> cans have the means to protect themselves in this age of terror. I will be
> always defending the Second Amendment.[72]

Second, Trump displayed his compassion and care for the LGBTQ
community:

> It's a strike at the heart and soul of who we are as a nation. It's an assault
> on the ability of free people to live their lives, love who they want, and
> express their identity. It's an attack on the right of every single American
> to live in peace and safety in their country.[73]

He also tweeted, "Thank you to the LGBT community! I will fight for you
while Hillary brings in more people that will threaten your freedoms and
beliefs."[74] This support for the LGBTQ community is not typical Republican rhetoric. Nevertheless, Trump demonstrated that at that time this specific
community was on his "good" side of moral duality and deserved his sympathy and patronage.

This division of people into a strict duality of "good" or "bad" has assisted
Trump with labeling his opponents as "evil," while at the same time representing himself and the institutions he supports positively. Employing voters'
anger, fear, and anxiety about threats to their security, he presents Democratic
leaders as incapable of protecting people from their concerns. On the other
hand, Trump demonstrates a deep connection with his supporters, which is
premised on shared empathy. Trump represents himself as the true protector
of American values, as the only protector who can save these values and the
American way of life. As one of the contestants of *The Apprentice* stated,
"If he likes you, he is warm and funny and charismatic and lovely. And if
he doesn't like you, just get out of the room. He is not nice to people that he
does not like."[75]

Trump has displayed fierce attitudes and has proposed severe measures to
deal with groups he perceives as threatening the American way of life, but at

the same time he shows support for people who like him. When a fan of *The Apprentice*, a young boy dying from cancer, asked Trump simply to tell him, "You're fired!", Trump wrote the boy a check for several thousand dollars and told him, "Go and have the time of your life."[76] When Melissa Young, a participant in the Miss USA pageant in 2005 was hospitalized with an incurable terminal illness, Trump sent her a note over an autographed photo: "To one of the bravest women I know. Best wishes." She reminded Trump about his support at one of his rallies, noting, "I just want to thank you. You saved me in so many ways." After learning that she was still sick, Trump came from the stage to hug her. "Hopefully, you're going to be around. Those doctors are going to be so wrong. It's heartbreaking, but something beautiful is gonna happen. You watch."[77]

Such behavior resonates well with Trump supporters. They see him as fair and just and are ready to overlook his toughness, especially if it is directed toward people they dislike. As one supporter stated, "He may be rough around the edges, but no one can say he doesn't say what he really thinks."[78] Others supporters have emphasized his moral qualities over his biased treatment of other groups. As one supporter stated, "He's raised some wonderful children, and that tells you a lot about a person."[79]

Such dual thinking represents the imperial stage of moral development.[80] The central value of this stage of development is defined by the needs of a person and the group. People at this stage of moral development clearly know what they need and are ready to fight for their freedom, power, and independence. They are however, unwilling to understand the feelings or motivations of others and do not want to listen to their needs and ideas. They see other people only in relation to their own needs and assess them in term of the extent to which they either do, or do not, meet their needs, fulfill their wishes, or help them to pursue their interests. Thus, to address their needs, people want to control the behavior of others. Trump promotes this form of morality by addressing the direct needs of his supporters at the expense of the needs of other people and groups. Similarly, his understanding of power rests on an unwavering commitment to an "us"-"them" duality, as we will see in the next chapter.

Notes

1. Arendt, Hannah. *The Human Condition.* Chicago: University of Chicago Press, 1958; Bataille, Georges. *Literature and Evil, trans. Alastair Hamilton*, 1st ed. Marion Boyars Publishers Ltd, 2001; Benhabib, Seyla. *The Reluctant Modernism of Hannah Arendt.* Rowman & Littlefield Publishers, 2003.
2. Alexander, Jeffrey C. "Citizen and Enemy as Symbolic Classification: On the Polarizing Discourse of Civil Society," in *Cultivating Differences: Symbolic Boundaries and the Making of Inequality,* ed. M Fournier and M Lamont. Chicago

University Press, (1992): 289–308; Alexander, Jeffrey C. *The Meanings of Social Life: A Cultural Sociology*. Oxford, USA: Oxford University Press.2003; Alexander, Jeffrey C. "Cultural pragmatics: Social performance between ritual and strategy." *Sociological Theory* 22, no. 4 (2004): 527–573; Edles, Laura D. *Symbol and Ritual in the New Spain: The Transition to Democracy after Franco.* Cambridge: Cambridge University Press, 1998; Magnuson, Eric, "Ideological conflict in American political culture: The discourse of civil society and American national narratives in American history textbooks." *International Journal of Sociology and Social Policy* 17, no. 6 (1997): 84–130; Smith, Philip. "Barbarism and Civility in the Discourses of Fascism, Communism, and Democracy: Variations on a Set of Themes." *Real civil societies* (1998): 115–137.

3. Smith, Philip. "Barbarism and civility in the discourses of fascism, communism, and democracy: Variations on a set of themes." *Real Civil Societies* (1998): 115–137.

4. Schudson, Michael. "The present in the past versus the past in the present." *Communication* 11, (1989): 105–113.

5. Auerbach, Yehudith. "The reconciliation pyramid—a narrative-based framework for analyzing identity conflicts." *Political Psychology* 30, no. 2 (2009): 291–318; Cobb. "Fostering Coexistence in Identity-Based Conflicts: Towards a Narrative Approach," *in Imagine Coexistence*. San Francisco: Jossey Bass, 2004: 294–310.

6. Pew Research Center Staff. "Partisan Polarization Surges in Bush, Obama Years," *Pew Research Center: U.S. Politics & Policy*, June 4, 2016, accessed June 10, 2016, http://www.people-press.org/2012/06/04/partisan-polarization-surges-in-bush-obama-years/

7. Doherty, Carroll. "Which Party Is More to Blame for Political Polarization? It Depends on the Measure," *Pew Research Center*, June 17, 2016, accessed June 17, 2016, http://www.pewresearch.org/fact-tank/2014/06/17/which-party-is-more-to-blame-for-political-polarization-it-depends-on-the-measure/

8. Tesler, Michael. "Democrats Increasingly Think the Confederate Flag is Racist: Republicans Don't," *the Washington Post*, July 9, 2015, accessed June 13, 2016, https://www.washingtonpost.com/blogs/monkey-cage/wp/2015/07/09/democrats-increasingly-think-the-confederate-flag-is-racist-republicans-dont/?action=click&contentCollection=meter-links-click&contentId=&mediaId=&module=meter-Links&pgtype=article&priority=true&referrer=&version=meter%20at%206

9. Swanson, Ana. "These Political Scientists may have just Discovered why U.S. Politics Are a Disaster," *The Washington Post*, October 7, 2015, accessed June 11, 2016, https://www.washingtonpost.com/news/wonk/wp/2015/10/07/these-political-scientists-may-have-discovered-the-real-reason-u-s-politics-are-a-disaster/

10. Pew Research Center Staff. "Partisan Polarization Surges in Bush, Obama Years."

11. Doherty, "Which Party Is More to Blame for Political Polarization?"

12. Desilver, Drew. "The Polarized Congress of Today Has Its Roots in the 1970s," *Pew Research Center*, June 12, 2014, accessed June 17, 2016, http://www.pewresearch.org/fact-tank/2014/06/12/polarized-politics-in-congress-began-in-the-1970s-and-has-been-getting-worse-ever-since/

13. Vavreck, Lynn. "American Anger: It's Not the Economy. It's the Other Party," *New York Times*, April 2, 2016, accessed June 17, 2016, http://www.nytimes.

com/2016/04/03/upshot/american-anger-its-not-the-economy-its-the-other-party.html

14. Tesler, Michael. "Democrats Increasingly Think the Confederate Flag Is Racist. Republicans Don't," *The Washington Post*, July 9, 2015, accessed June 18, 2016, https://www.washingtonpost.com/blogs/monkey-cage/wp/2015/07/09/democrats-increasingly-think-the-confederate-flag-is-racist-republicans-dont/?action=click&contentCollection=meter-links-click&contentId=&mediaId=&module=meter-Links&pgtype=article&priority=true&referrer=&version=meter%20at%206

15. YouGov. "Favorability of Flag: Do You Have a Favorable or an Unfavorable Opinion of the Confederate Flag?" *YouGov*, June 23–25, 2016, accessed June 18, 2016, https://d25d2506sfb94s.cloudfront.net/cumulus_uploads/document/jntynmhast/tabs_OPI_confederate_flag_20150625.pdf

16. Pew Research Center Staff. "Views of Impact of Global Economic Involvement Policies toward Developing Countries," *Pew Research Center: U.S. Politics & Policy*, May 5, 2016, accessed June 13, 2016 http://www.people-press.org/2016/05/05/2-views-of-impact-of-global-economic-involvement-policies-toward-developing-countries/

17. Doherty, C. "Which Party Is More to Blame for Political Polarization?"

18. Iyengar, Shanto, Gaurav Sood, and Yphtach Lelkes. "Affect, not ideology a social identity perspective on polarization." *Public opinion quarterly* 76, no. 3 (2012): 405–431.

19. Tesler, "Democrats Increasingly Think the Confederate Flag is Racist."

20. Frum, "The Great Republican Revolt."

21. World Values Survey, accessed June 19, 2016, http://www.worldvaluessurvey.org/wvs.jsp

22. Kahn, Chris. "Exclusive: Top Reason Americans Will Vote for Trump: 'To Stop Clinton'—Poll," *Reuters*, May 9, 2016, accessed June 10, 2016, http://www.reuters.com/article/us-usa-election-anti-vote-idUSKCN0XX06E

23. Doherty, "Which Party Is More to Blame for Political Polarization?"

24. Kahn, C. "Exclusive."

25. Bykowicz and Pace. "Never Mind Trump."

26. Bump, Philip. "How Likely Are Bernie Sanders Supporters to Actually Vote for Donald Trump? Here Are Some Clues," *The Washington Post*, May 24, 2016, accessed June 11, 2016 https://www.washingtonpost.com/news/the-fix/wp/2016/05/24/how-likely-are-bernie-sanders-supporters-to-actually-vote-for-donald-trump-here-are-some-clues/

27. Strether, Lambert. "2:00pm Water Cooler 5/10/2016," *Naked Capitalism*, May 10, 2016, accessed June 12, 2016, http://www.nakedcapitalism.com/2016/05/200pm-water-cooler-5102016.html#comment-2594221

28. Smith, Yves. "Why Some of the Smartest Progressives I Know will Vote for Trump over Hillary," *Politico*, June 1, 2016, accessed June 11, 2016, http://www.politico.com/magazine/story/2016/06/wall-street-2016-donald-trump-hillary-clinton-213931#ixzz4BZXv64UE

29. Martin, Jonathan, and Dalia Sussman. "Republicans Want Their Party to Unite Behind Donald Trump, Poll Shows," *New York Times*, May 19, 2016, accessed June 4, 2016, http://www.nytimes.com/2016/05/20/us/politics/donald-trump-hillary-clinton-poll.html

30. Ibid.

31. Johnson, Melinda. "Paul Ryan's Endorsement of Donald Trump: What They're Saying," *Syracuse*, June 3, 2016, accessed (date needed), http://www.syracuse.

com/opinion/index.ssf/2016/06/paul_ryans_endorsement_of_trump_what_theyre_saying.html

32. The Washington Times Staff. "Yes, Republicans Are Uniting (and the #NEV-ERTRUMP Movement Is Dead)," *The Washington Times*, June 2, 2016, accessed June 4, 2016, http://www.donaldjtrump.com/media/yes-republicans-are-uniting-and-the-nevertrump-movement-is-dead
33. Gingrich, Newt. *Twitter*, accessed June 18, 2016 https://mobile.twitter.com/newtgingrich?ref_src=twsrc%5Etfw
34. Trump, Donald. J. *The America We Deserve.*
35. Trump, Donald. J. *Great Again: How to Fix Our Crippled America*, Threshold Editions, 2015 p.116.
36. Santucci, John, and Meghan Keneally. "NRA Endorses Donald Trump for President," *ABC News*, May 20, 2016, accessed June 3, 2016, http://abcnews.go.com/Politics/nra-endorse-donald-trump-president/story?id=39253893
37. Bykowicz and Pace. "Never Mind Trump."
38. Santucci, John, and Meghan Keneally. "NRA Endorses Donald Trump for President," *ABC News*, May 20, 2016, accessed June 3, 2016, http://abcnews.go.com/Politics/nra-endorse-donald-trump-president/story?id=39253893
39. Liah, Greenfeld, and Daniel Chirot. "Nationalism and aggression." *Theory and Society* 23, no. 1 (1994): 79–130.
40. Eisenstadt, Shmuel Noah, ed. *Comparative Civilizations and Multiple Modernities*. Brill, Vol. 1, 2003; Kern, Thomas. "Cultural performance and political regime change." *Sociological Theory* 27, no. 3 (September 2009): 291–316.
41. Kern, Thomas. "Cultural performance and political regime change." *Sociological Theory* 27, no. 3 (2009): 291–316.
42. March 14, 2016 issue of *Time*.
43. Rees, "What 18 Former *Apprentice* Candidates Really Think of Donald Trump."
44. Our Story, Women Vote Trump, accessed June 19, 2016, http://womenvotetrump.com
45. January 18, 2016 issue of *Time*.
46. February 22, 2016 issue of *Time*.
47. Office of the Press Secretary. "Remarks by the President after Briefing on the Attack in Orlando," *The White House: Office of the Press Secretary*, June 13, 2016, accessed June 11, 2016, https://www.whitehouse.gov/the-press-office/2016/06/13/remarks-president-after-briefing-attack-orlando-florida
48. Cohen, Roger. "Orlando and Trump's America," *New York Times*, June 13, 2016, accessed June 14, 2016, http://www.nytimes.com/2016/06/14/opinion/orlando-omar-mateen-pulse-florida-donald-trumps-america.html
49. Liptak, Keven and Stephen Collinson. "Obama Goes on Tirade against Trump Over 'Dangerous' Muslim Ban. 'Radical Islam,'" *CNN Politics*, June 14, 2016, accessed June 14, 2016, http://www.cnn.com/2016/06/14/politics/obama-pushes-back-against-criticism-over-terrorism-rhetoric/
50. Trump, Donald J. "Appreciate the congrats from being right on radical Islamic terrorism, I don't want congrats, I want toughness & vigilance. We must be smart," *Twitter*, June 12, 2016, accessed June 14, 2016, https://mobile.twitter.com/realDonaldTrump/status/742034549232766976
51. Reinhard, Beth, and Reid J. Epstein. "Donald Trump Goes On Offense, Blaming President," *The Wall Street Journal*, June 13, 2016, accessed June 14, 2016, http://www.wsj.com/articles/donald-trump-broadens-proposal-to-ban-muslim-immigrants-1465849074

52. Martin, Jonathan, and Alexander Burns. "Blaming Muslims After Attack, Donald Trump Tosses Pluralism Aside," *New York Times*, June 13, 2016, accessed June 14, 2016, http://www.nytimes.com/2016/06/14/us/politics/donald-trump-hillary-clinton-speeches.html?_r=1
53. Berenson, Tessa. "Donald Trump Pushes for Muslim Ban After Orlando Shooting," *Time*, June 13, 2016, accessed June 14, 2016, http://time.com/4366912/donald-trump-orlando-shooting-muslim-ban/
54. Reinhard and Epstein. "Donald Trump Goes on Offense, Blaming President."
55. Berenson, "Donald Trump Pushes for Muslim Ban After Orlando Shooting."
56. New York Times Staff. "Donald Trump Seizes on Orlando Shooting and Repeats Call for Temporary Ban on Muslim Migration," *Donald J Trump: Trump Make American Great Again*, June 12, 2016, accessed June 14, 2016, http://www.donaldjtrump.com/media/donald-trump-seizes-on-orlando-shooting-and-repeats-call-for-temporary-ban
57. Rothbart, Daniel, and Karina V. Korostelina, eds. *Identity, Morality, and Threat: Studies in Violent Conflict*. Lexington, MA: Lexington Books, 2006; Rothbart, Daniel and Karina V. Korostelina, *Why They Die: Civilian Devastation in Violent Conflict*. University of Michigan Press, 2011.
58. Ibid.
59. Rothbart, Daniel, and Karina. V. Korostelina. *Why They Die: Civilian Devastation in Violent Conflict*. University of Michigan Press, 2011.
60. Ibid., 46.
61. Ibid., 49.
62. Memoli, Michael. A. "Paul Ryan Stands Firm against Trump's Proposed Ban on Muslim Immigration," *The Los Angeles Times*, June 14, 2016, accessed June 16, 2016 http://www.latimes.com/politics/la-na-trailguide-paul-ryan-stands-firm-against-trump-s-1465918852-htmlstory.html
63. Reuters. "Donald Trump's Proposed Muslim Ban is Likley Illegal But. . ." *Newsweek*, June 14, 2016, accessed June 15, 2016, http://www.newsweek.com/donald-trump-muslims-ban-terrorism-radical-islam-guns-orlando-shooting-legal-470470
64. Reinhard and Epstein. "Donald Trump Goes On Offense, Blaming President."
65. Flynn, Mike. "Reuters: Half of Likely Voters Back Temporary Ban on all Muslim Entry to United States," *Breitbart*, June 14, 2016, accessed June 14, 2016, http://www.breitbart.com/2016-presidential-race/2016/06/14/reuters-half-likely-voters-want-temporarily-ban-muslims-us/
66. Wong, Kristina. "Poll: Half of American voters back Trump's Muslim ban," *The Hill*, March 29, 2016, accessed June 15,2016, http://thehill.com/policy/defense/274521-poll-half-of-american-voters-back-trumps-muslim-ban
67. Khalid, Asma. "Are GOP Women Warming Up to Donald Trump," *NPR*, June 15, 2016, accessed June 17, 2016, http://www.npr.org/2016/06/15/482113672/are-gop-women-warming-up-to-trump
68. New York Times Staff. "Donald Trump seizes on Orlando Shooting."
69. Murchison, William. "Trump Trumps on Orlando," *RealClear Politics*, June 14, 2016, accessed June 14, 2016, http://www.realclearpolitics.com/articles/2016/06/14/trump_trumps_on_orlando_130880.html
70. New York Times Staff. "Donald Trump seizes on Orlando Shooting."
71. Berenson, "Donald Trump Pushes for Muslim Ban After Orlando Shooting."
72. Hawkins, Awr. "Donald Trump: I Will Consult NRA on How Americans Can Defend Themselves," *Breitbart*, June 13, 2016, accessed June 14, 2016,

http://www.breitbart.com/big-government/2016/06/13/donald-trump-i-will-consult-nra-on-how-americans-can-defend-themselves/

73. Berenson, "Donald Trump Pushes for Muslim Ban After Orlando Shooting."
74. Trump, Donald. J. "Donald J. Trump @realDonaldTrump," accessed June 15, 2016, https://mobile.twitter.com/realDonaldTrump?ref_src=twsrc%5Egoogle%7Ctwcamp%5Eserp%7Ctwgr%5Eauthor
75. Rees, "What 18 Former *Apprentice* Candidates Really Think of Donald Trump."
76. McAdams, Dan. P. "The Mind of Donald Trump," *The Atlantic*, June 2016, accessed June 28, 2016, http://www.theatlantic.com/magazine/archive/2016/06/the-mind-of-donald-trump/480771/
77. Chapman, Steve. "The Big Difference between Donald Trump and Hilary Clinton," *Chicago Tribune*, March 30, 2016, accessed June 3, 2016, http://www.chicagotribune.com/news/opinion/chapman/ct-donald-trump-hillary-clinton-personalities-chapman-0331-jm-20160330-column.html
78. "Candidates."*Inside Gov by Graphiq*, accessed June 6, 2016, http://presidential-candidates.insidegov.com/compare/40–70/Hillary-Clinton-vs-Donald-Trump
79. Khalid, Asma. "Are GOP Women Warming Up to Donald Trump," *NPR*, June 15, 2016, accessed June 17, 2016, http://www.npr.org/2016/06/15/482113672/are-gop-women-warming-up-to-trump
80. Kegan, Robert. *The Evolving Self: Problem and Process in Human Development.* Cambridge, MA: Harvard University Press, 1982.

7 Making America Great Again

The idea of power is central to the political life of any nation. However, understandings of what power is differ significantly among politicians and their followers. Power has been classically defined as the ability of one person or group to influence the behavior of others as well as impede or support the ability of others to achieve their objectives.[1] A group or individual in power can, thus, create the conditions in which subordinate groups feel inspired and empowered to accomplish their goals. Conversely, a more powerful group can also create the conditions in which subordinate groups feel inadequate and ill equipped to deal with their current circumstances in order to satisfy their needs. This dual influence depends greatly upon the degree of power exercised within the existing socio-political system by various groups: the system defines which actions carried out by people in power are acceptable and legitimate. Pertinently, the influence exerted by a powerful person or group is heightened in times of national stress and uncertainty.

A person or group in power can possess two sets of values, which they perceive to be important. Welfare values pertain to gaining wealth and access to resources, in addition to specific skills. Deference values lead people to place greater emphasis on the legitimacy and reputation of different leaders and groups in society, including whether these individuals and groups are to be respected. People in power can use both welfare and deference values to control and influence the behavior of their followers and others with a lower status. Those not in positions of authority are, thus, dependent upon leaders to satisfy their needs and desires, or, indeed, fulfill their goals. Exerting power over people also involves both a population being dependent on those in power and those in power coercing a populace. Leaders can bend people's will and beliefs by establishing norms and creating a degree of forced or accepted social consensus.[2]

This concept of power presents itself as something which is "given," as self-perpetuating, durable, and hard to overturn or to alter by people who occupy positions of dependency. These groups and individuals are dependent upon the goodwill and support of government in any hierarchical socio-political system. This approach to power is premised on the ability of leaders to enforce their particular system of social and political interactions despite resistance from opponents and the people.[3] More specifically, this can be achieved through the development of specific political ideologies created by leaders and the promotion of particular social practices.[4] Rulers establish specific symbols that give meaning to social situations and, thus, define the actions and behavior of people.[5]

Alternatively, the liberal concept of power introduces power as something fragile.[6] Governments do not possess power but are rather dependent on the will of the people. To function effectively, government needs the support of its citizenry in order to exercise legitimate political authority and implement policies. In line with this concept, rulers, therefore, have two types of resources at their disposal. The first comprises authority as a right to command and be obeyed, inclusive of access to the necessary material resources and sanctions in order to lead. The second pertains to human resources—people who obey a ruler—and intangible factors: their habits and attitudes toward submission, the popularity of an existing political ideology, a common faith, and shared vision of the nation. These resources depend on the obedience and cooperation of populations and their contributions to the established system.[7]

Central to this understanding of power are societal interactions—people speaking and acting "in concert."[8] More specifically, power is considered an essential characteristic of the social relations among individuals within a community who exercise their power through communication and cooperation.[9] This form of power is productive; it gives people an initial ability to act and to be empowered, and it develops resistance to existing structures of power or alternative symbolic systems.[10] Therefore, people have more power when they work jointly and in solidarity.[11] This conceptualization of power as creative collaboration[12] includes persuasion, the ability to convince people of the rightness of a particular order, and a shared belief in the validity of a particular leader.[13]

Trump grasps well the dissatisfaction among his would-be supporters with this liberal interpretation of power. Moreover, he has sought to heighten this dissatisfaction by presenting this form of power relations as weak and ultimately doomed to fail. He associates this cooperative form of power with politicians who promote globalization and multiculturalism, and has positioned himself as an alternative, anti-establishment figure. As one supporter stated, "I like him because he is to the point, and it's time for a change, I think he's got the oomph to rattle some cages."[14]

Trump, therefore, is reinvigorating the once outdated perception of power as a zero-sum game that is reliant on dominance, coercion, and competition. In order to increase the power of the U.S. and change the existing power imbalance in the international system, Trump has continually emphasized throughout his campaign that this requires denying other groups and countries access to resources. More specifically, he has promised to make America great again by reducing the power of other countries. He has advocated for cutting American support for allies such as Germany and Japan who have been portrayed by Trump as free riders. He has sought to capitalize on the popular opinion among Americans that international trade has taken American jobs and know-how out of the country and the belief that immigration is ruining America. Each one of these proposed policies involves scaling back the resources given to other countries in order to reduce their overall power rather than increasing the capacity of the U.S. directly. Trump supporters have gladly accepted this zero-sum perception of power because it resonates with their understanding of strength.

Trump favors a strong, dominant, and even authoritarian style of leadership. He praised the Russian president Vladimir Putin: "He's running his country, and at least he's a leader, unlike what we have in this country."[15] Although Trump has demonstrated a preference for Putin's style of leadership in comparison with Obama's, he did stress he "absolutely" condemns the alleged killing of journalists by the Russian president.[16] Several months after his interview in which he referred to Putin, Trump uploaded a campaign video to his official Instagram account presenting both the Russian leader and ISIS as enemies of America. The video also depicted Hilary Clinton as a barking dog.[17] Trump often stresses: "Our jobs are being sucked away, our military can't beat ISIS . . . our borders are like Swiss cheese."[18] He believes powerful leadership requires a tougher response to the problems currently facing the U.S., which embraces the use of coercive force. This approach utilizes domination and force to challenge the weakening position of America in the globalized world and the tendency toward international cooperation, and the existing ineffective strategies to combat terrorism.

America in a Globalized World

The American public holds several different attitudes toward globalization. Republicans and Republican-leaning voters who back Donald Trump are the most skeptical of U.S. involvement in the global economy. Sixty-five percent of them believe it has a negative effect on America. They strongly oppose the current approach to engagement with developing nations: 78 percent of them are against increasing foreign aid to developing nations, 67 percent oppose importing more goods from these nations, and 63 percent disapprove of increasing U.S. companies' investment abroad.[19]

A majority of Americans believe the national interests of the U.S. should come first before international involvement. Fifty-seven percent of Americans want the U.S. "to deal with its own problems and let other countries deal with their own problems the best they can." Only 37 percent say the U.S. "should help other countries deal with their problems." Similarly 69 percent of Americans agree the U.S. "should concentrate more on our own national problems." This tendency is stronger among Republicans: 73 percent of them believe the U.S. should focus more on domestic issues and less on international problems. Assessing the role of the next president, 70 percent of Americans say it is more important to focus on domestic policy than foreign policy.[20]

Trump has echoed these sentiments shared by his supporters and has emphasized the importance of regaining control over globalization processes. Trump's approach to power as coercion is presented as more suited to the U.S. than the more liberal and cooperative approach of the Obama-Clinton administration: "Hillary Clinton and her friends in global finance want to scare America into thinking small—and they want to scare the American people out of voting for a better future. My campaign has the opposite message."[21]

In his speech "How to Make America Wealthy Again" in Pennsylvania in June 2016, Trump painted globalization in a dark light: "Globalization has made the financial elite who donate to politicians very, very wealthy . . . but it's left millions of our workers with nothing but poverty and heartache."[22] He described current trade agreements—Trans-Pacific Partnership (TPP), a twelve-nation trade deal among the U.S. and Pacific Rim countries promoted by President Barack Obama, and the North American Free Trade Agreement (NAFTA) with Canada and Mexico—as "failed trade policies." Trump told his audience he would reject the agreements or renegotiate them from a position of power. Trump said he would

> appoint the toughest and smartest trade negotiators to fight on behalf of American workers . . . And I don't mean just a little bit better, I mean a lot better. If they do not agree to a renegotiation, then I will submit notice under Article 2205 of the NAFTA agreement that America intends to withdraw from the deal.[23]

He has also promised to actively pursue the punishment of countries violating trade rules. One of his first orders of business would be to have the secretary of commerce identify foreign countries in violation of trade regulations, which are harming American workers, and use all legal tactics to end such practices.

Trump has specifically vowed to practice a tough approach toward China. During his announcement speech for the presidency on June 16, 2015, Trump offered an unconventional approach to the issue of China:

> When was the last time you heard China is killing us? They're devaluing their currency to a level that you wouldn't believe. It makes it impossible

for our companies to compete, impossible. They're killing us. But you don't hear that from anybody else.[24]

Speaking in Pennsylvania on June 27, 2016, he promised to label China as a currency manipulator. "China's unfair subsidy behavior is prohibited by the terms of its entrance to the WTO, and I intend to enforce those rules,"[25] Trump said. He also proposed to increase tariffs on Chinese imports coming into the U.S.[26]

Trump's critical view of globalization was reaffirmed following the results of the UK's referendum to leave the European Union. In his official statement, Trump praised this vote as a victory for the country and the triumph of the idea of independence: "The people of the United Kingdom have exercised the sacred right of all free peoples. They have declared their independence from the European Union and have voted to reassert control over their own politics, borders and economy."[27] Explaining that the vote was a result of people's resentment, he said,

I think it's a great thing that's happened. It's an amazing vote, very historic. People are angry all over the world. They're angry over borders, they're angry over people coming into the country and taking over and nobody even knows who they are. They're angry about many, many things in the UK, the U.S. and many other places. This will not be the last. [28]

He pointed to the similarities in people's attitudes to globalization in both the UK and the U.S.: "I think I see a big parallel—people want to take their country back."[29] Trump also stressed he and his supporters were on the right track for the U.S.: "Basically, they took back their country. That's a great thing. I think we're doing very well in the United States also, and it is essentially the same thing that is happening in the United States."[30] Moreover, Trump used this opportunity to emphasize once again his disagreement with Clinton's approach to power:

I was on the right side of that issue—with the people—while Hillary, as always, stood with the elites, and both she and President Obama predicted that one wrong. Now it's time for the American people to take back their future. That's the choice we face. We can either give in to Hillary Clinton's campaign of fear, or we can choose to believe in America.[31]

Trump rejects globalization as cooperation and increased political and economic interconnectivity, which empowers and promotes the development of all partners involved. Instead, he endorses the idea of taking control over the processes of globalization and coercing partners into agreements that will benefit America first. He sees the future of America not in developing international cooperation with other nations but in dominating the international sphere and promoting the national interest of the country. This approach to global power resonates well with his supporters. In dealing with trade agreements with other countries, American voters give the GOP an eleven-point lead over the Democratic Party.[32] As one Trump supporter stated, "I think we should not allow our companies to manufacture overseas. I hope Trump can find ways to stop it." [33]

The Position of America within the International Arena

The American public is critical about the role the U.S. plays in the world. Forty-one percent of Americans believe the U.S. does too much to solve world problems, whereas only 27 percent say it does too little. This difference is even stronger for Republicans: 67 percent of them say U.S. policies should be aimed at keeping the U.S. as the sole superpower. Forty-three percent of Republicans believe the NATO alliance is more beneficial for other member states than for the U.S., and 52 percent of them say the U.S. should pursue its own interests, even if allies strongly object.

Many Americans believe that under the Obama administration the U.S. is losing its superior position in the world: 61 percent of Americans, including 71 percent of Republicans believe America is respected less by other countries.[34] As one Trump supporter stated, "In my opinion, Obama is the most anti-American president that I have experienced. He bows down to every other country. He puts other countries before America."[35]

Trump has echoed these sentiments, stressing Obama's domestic and foreign policy strategies have not been effective nor successful:

> President Obama has weakened our military by weakening our economy. He's crippled us with wasteful spending, massive debt, low growth, a huge trade deficit and open borders . . . He negotiated a disastrous deal with Iran, and then we watched them ignore its terms, even before the ink was dry.[36]

He has criticized President Obama's approach to international relations, depicting his reliance on international cooperation that undermines America's leadership role as weakness. "We're just—you know, we have a president, frankly, that doesn't—nobody is afraid of our president. Nobody respects our president. You take a look at what's going on throughout the world. It's not the country that it was."[37] Trump has also emphasized how Obama's view on international cooperation has led foreign powers to increasingly disrespect the U.S and the institute of the presidency, citing such events as Obama's arrival in Cuba and Saudi Arabia where he was not greeted at the airport by either country's leadership, as well as the inability of Obama to deal with North Korea and China. In his foreign policy speech on April 27, 2016, Trump stated, "If President Obama's goal had been to weaken America, he could not have done a better job."[38]

Trump has also sought to address the concerns of the American public regarding the current position of America in the world by proposing a different approach to international relations: "from a position of strength."[39] At a rally in Nevada, Trump restated his preference for dominance over cooperation: "What do we all want? We want security. We want a strong country."[40] He believes a better world is not based on cooperation among equals but rather on the strength of the U.S.: "The world is most peaceful, and most prosperous, when America is strongest."[41]

Trump has continually emphasized how countries around the world abuse the assistance of the U.S. in order to maintain their security, and they do not provide their fair share in return:

> "We are supporting nations now, militarily, we are supporting nations like Saudi Arabia . . . We are supporting them, militarily, and they pay us a fraction, a fraction of what they should be paying us and of the cost. We are supporting Japan. Most people didn't even know that. Most people didn't know that we are taking care of Japan's military needs."[42]

Trump continued, "We're rebuilding other countries while weakening our own."[43]

He believes this policy of international aid makes America look weak: "Our allies must contribute toward the financial, political and human costs of our tremendous security burden. But many of them are simply not doing so. They look at the United States as weak and forgiving and feel no obligation to honor their agreements with us."[44] Trump has vowed to change the existing balance of power and to promote American dominance, stating,

> We're protecting all of these nations all over the world. We can't afford to do it anymore . . . they have to protect themselves or they have to pay us. Here's the thing, with Japan, they have to pay us or we have to let them protect themselves.[45]

Trump has also been critical of American's participation in international alliances. More specifically, he has a particularly unfavorable opinion of NATO. Trump noted how useless and irresponsible U.S. spending on NATO has been and has advocated for shifting the focus toward domestic problems instead:

> NATO is obsolete . . . We're spending a tremendous—billions and billions of dollars on NATO. . . We're paying too much! You have countries

in NATO, I think it's 28 countries—you have countries in NATO that
are getting a free ride and it's unfair, it's very unfair. The United States
cannot afford to be the policemen of the world anymore, folks. We have
to rebuild our own country.[46]

To that end, Trump has proposed a review of current NATO agreements
and a redefinition of the goals and strategies pursued by the alliance: "We
will discuss how we can upgrade NATO's outdated mission and structure—
grown out of the Cold War—to confront our shared challenges, including
migration and Islamic terrorism."[47]

Dealing with Terrorism

Americans believe the government is not doing enough to protect them
against acts of terror. Eighty percent of the public, including 93 percent
of Republicans, say ISIS is a major threat to the well-being of the U.S.[48]
A majority of Republicans (77 percent) believe Islam is more likely than
other religions to promote violence.[49]

Sixty-two percent of Americans approve of the U.S. military campaign
against Islamic militants in Iraq and Syria but largely criticize the current
actions of the government. Republicans are particularly negative in their
assessment of the campaign: only 29 percent of them believe the government is doing very or fairly well reducing the threat of terrorism. Sixty-eight
percent of Republicans say the U.S. effort is not going well, and 74 percent are concerned the U.S. will not go far enough to stop militants. Sixty-
eight percent of Republicans support sending ground troops to fight ISIS in
Iraq and Syria, and 70 percent believe military force is the best approach to
defeating global terrorism. Republicans are not particularly concerned about
the methods used to fight terrorism, inclusive of torture. For 64 percent of
Republicans, protecting the country takes precedence over civil liberties, and
only 23 percent stress the importance of restrictions on torture. Additionally,
80 percent of conservative Republicans and 61 percent of moderate and liberal Republicans view the large number of refugees leaving such countries as
Iraq and Syria as a major threat.[50]

Trump caters to these views and has sought to address these concerns.
Trump has been skeptical about Obama's and Clinton's response to recent
terrorist attacks that emphasized the importance of solidarity as a way to
counter terrorism. According to Clinton, dealing with the threat of terrorism
requires the U.S. to "deepen . . . cooperation with . . . allies and partners in
the Middle East. Such cooperation is essential to protecting the homeland
and keeping our country safe."[51] Trump, however, has criticized this position

toward terrorism and the opposition to torture as a means to gain critical information as weak and ineffective:

> Can you imagine them sitting around the table or wherever they're eating their dinner, talking about the Americans don't do waterboarding and yet we chop off heads? They probably think we're weak, we're stupid, we don't know what we're doing, we have no leadership.[52]

Instead, Trump has proposed a tough policy of broad and forceful measures against terrorists and enemy combatants. Shortly after the attacks at Istanbul's Ataturk Airport that killed thirty-six people, Trump tweeted, "Will the world ever realize what is going on? So sad."[53] Later that day in his speech in Ohio, he described his approach to terrorism: "You have to fight fire with fire. We have to be so strong. We have to fight so viciously. And violently because we're dealing with violent people viciously."[54] Trump went further, noting this approach should have no restriction. Referring to the practice of waterboarding, which Trump referred to as "not the nicest thing," he nevertheless advocated for its use in dealing with the enemy. He previously supported the use of waterboarding during a March 3 Republican presidential debate in Detroit: "We should go for waterboarding and we should go tougher than waterboarding."[55] He also confirmed his view at a rally at Dayton airport: "I'm 100 percent fine with waterboarding . . . and it should be increased."[56]

Throughout his campaign, Trump has vowed to protect America from terrorism internationally and domestically. He has promised to bolster America's defense: "I will build a military so strong that we'll never have to use it because they are going to be saying, 'I'm not going to mess with that guy.'"[57] He has also pledged to defend the homeland from radical Islam: "There are scores of recent migrants inside our borders charged with terrorism. For every case known to the public, there are dozens more. We must stop importing extremism through senseless immigration policies."[58]

This approach resonates strongly with Trump supporters. Forty-six percent of the American public believes the Republican Party could do a better job addressing the terrorist threat in the U.S., whereas 37 percent say the Democratic Party could do the better job.[59] Americans believe that Trump would handle terrorism and homeland security better than Clinton with a margin of 44 percent to 39 percent.[60] Geist, a military contractor who fought in Benghazi and co-authored *13 Hours: The Inside Account of What Really Happened in Benghazi*, endorsed Trump in February, saying he believed "under President Trump, many conflicts will be avoided because our enemies will fear the United States and our military."[61]

Trump's approach to international and domestic policy is based on strength, pressure, and the repeal of current policies on immigration, refugees, and foreign aid. He does not value power achieved through cooperation among equals, but rather perceives powers as dominance over others. He believes he can use his authority not only to force others to comply but also to carry out his policies despite resistance from opponents and certain segments of the American public. Trump does not view power as dependent on people's goodwill but rather seeks to use it as a tool of coercion in order to pursue his goals, which include the punishment of those individuals and groups who do not support his cause. For example, he has suggested his former Republican primary rivals, who have declined to back him in November, should be barred from ever running for public office again.[62] This approach to power denies collaboration and the liberal interpretation of power as mutual enfranchisement. Rather, it promotes American domination on the international stage.

Notes

1. Cartwright, Dorwin. *Studies in Social Power*, Research Center for Group Dynamics, Institute for Social Research, University of Michigan, 1959; Deutsch, Morton, and Gerard, Harold B. "A study of normative and informational social influences upon individual judgment." *The Journal of Abnormal and Social Psychology*, 51, no. 3 (1955): 629–636; Festinger, L. "A theory of social comparison processes." *Human Relations*, 7, no. 2 (1954): 117–140; French, J. R. P., and B. Raven. "The Bases of Social Power," in *Studies in Social Power*, ed. Dorwin Cartwright. Research Center for Group Dynamics, Institute for Social Research, University of Michigan, 1959: 150–167.
2. Moscovici, Serge. *Social Influence and Social Change*, published in cooperation with European Association of Experimental Social Psychology by Academic Press, 1976.
3. Weber, Max. *Economy and Society: An Outline of Interpretive Sociology*, California: University of California Press, 1978.
4. Foucault, M. *The History of Sexuality*. Harmondsworth: Penguin Books, 1981.
5. Bourdieu, *Outline of a Theory of Practice*. Cambridge Studies in Social Anthropology 16. Cambridge, New York: Cambridge University Press, 1977.
6. Sharp, Gene. *The Politics of Nonviolent Action*, Boston: P. Sargent Publisher, 1973.
7. Ibid.
8. Arendt, Hannah. *The Human Condition*. Charles R. Walgreen Foundation Lectures. Chicago: University of Chicago Press, 1958; Arendt, Hannah. *On Violence*. New York: Harcourt, Brace & World, 1970.
9. Barnett, Michael N., and Raymond Duvall. *Power in Global Governance*. Cambridge, UK, NY: Cambridge University Press, 2005.
10. Foucault, M. *The History of Sexuality: An Introduction*. Vol. 1. New York: Vintage books, 1990; Bourdieu, Pierre, *Outline of a Theory of Practice*, Cambridge Studies in Social Anthropology 16. Cambridge; New York: Cambridge University Press, 1977.
11. Amy Allen. *The Power of Feminist Theory: Domination, Resistance, Solidarity.* Westview Press, 1999.

12. Boulding, K. E. *Three Faces of Power*, Newbury Park: Sage Publications, Inc, 1990.
13. Turner, John C. "Explaining the nature of power: A three-process theory." *European Journal of Social Psychology* 35, no.1 (2005): 1–22.
14. Edsall, Thomas B. "Measuring the Trump Effect," JUNE 16, 2016, accessed on July 7, 2016, http://www.nytimes.com/2016/06/16/opinion/campaign-stops/measuring-the-trump-effect.html?_r=0
15. Taylor, Adam. "The Complicated Reality behind Trump's Claim That There's No Proof Putin Had Journalists Killed," *Washington Post*, December 21, 2015, accessed (date needed), https://www.washingtonpost.com/news/worldviews/wp/2015/12/21/the-complicated-reality-behind-trumps-claim-that-theres-no-proof-putin-had-journalists-killed/
16. Ibid.
17. Trump, Donald, J. "When It Comes to Facing our Toughest Opponents . . . . ," accessed June 20, 2016, https://www.instagram.com/p/BDBS8bYGhWr/
18. Hulsey, Lynn. "Donald Trump Speaks to Thousands at Dayton Airport," *Dayton Daily News*, March 13, 2016, accessed June 21, 2016, http://www.daytondailynews.com/news/news/state-regional-govt-politics/donald-trump-in-dayton-saturday/nqfnG/
19. Pew Research Center. "Public Uncertain, Divided Over American's Place in the World."
20. Ibid.
21. McCaskill, Nolan. D,. and Eli Stokols. "Trump Trashes GOP Trade Agenda," *Politico*, June 28, 2016, accessed June 20, 2016, http://www.politico.com/story/2016/06/trump-jobs-plan-224892#ixzz4Cu8O3shL
22. Jackson, David. "Donald Trump Targets Globalization and Free Trade as Job Killers," *USA TODAY*, June 28, 2016, accessed June 21, 2016, http://www.usatoday.com/story/news/politics/elections/2016/06/28/donald-trump-globalization-trade-pennsylvania-ohio/86431376/
23. McCaskill, and Stokols. "Trump Trashes GOP Trade Agenda."
24. *Time* Staff. "Here's Donald Trump's Presidential Announcement Speech."
25. McCaskill, and Stokols. "Trump Trashes GOP Trade Agenda."
26. Jackson. "Donald Trump Targets Globalization and Free Trade as Job Killers."
27. https://www.donaldjtrump.com/press-releases/donald-j.-trump-statement-regarding-british-referendum-on-e.u.-membership
28. Sim, Philip. "Donald Trump in Scotland: 'Brexit a Great Thing,'" *BBC News: Glasgo & West Scotland*, June 24, 2016, accessed June 27, 2016, http://www.bbc.com/news/uk-scotland-glasgow-west-36606184
29. Bixby, Scott. "Donald Trump Hails Britain's Decision to Leave EU as It Happened," *The Guardian*, June 24, 2016, accessed June 27, 2016, https://www.theguardian.com/us-news/live/2016/jun/24/us-election-campaign-live-trump-scotland-sanders-clinton
30. Sim. "Donald Trump in Scotland."
31. McCaskill and Stokols. "Trump Trashes GOP Trade Agenda."
32. Pew Research Center. "Public Uncertain, Divided Over American's Place in the World."
33. Jackson. "Donald Trump Targets Globalization and Free Trade as Job Killers."
34. *Pew Research Center* "Public Uncertain, Divided Over American's Place in the World."

35. Winship, Scott. "Trumpism: 'It's the Culture, Stupid,'" *National Review*, March 15, 2016, accessed May 19, 2016, http://www.nationalreview.com/article/432822/donald-trump-culture-not-economy
36. Trump, Donald. J. "Donald J. Trump Foreign Policy Speech," *Trump: Make America Great Again!* April 27, 2016, accessed May 20, 2016, https://www.donaldjtrump.com/press-releases/donald-j.-trump-foreign-policy-speech
37. Cillizza, Chris. "Donald Trump Did a CNN Townhall Last Night, and It was a Classic," *The Washington Post*, accessed June 1, 2016, https://www.washingtonpost.com/news/the-fix/wp/2016/03/30/donald-trump-did-a-cnn-townhall-last-night-and-it-was-a-classic/
38. Trump. "Donald J. Trump Foreign Policy Speech."
39. Ibid.
40. Winship. "Trumpism."
41. Trump. "Donald J. Trump Foreign Policy Speech."
42. Cillizza. "Donald Trump Did a CNN Townhall Last Night."
43. Trump "Donald J. Trump Foreign Policy Speech."
44. Ibid.
45. Cillizza. "Donald Trump Did a CNN Townhall Last Night."
46. Ibid.
47. Trump. "Donald J. Trump Foreign Policy Speech."
48. Pew Research Center. "Public Uncertain, Divided Over American's Place in the World."
49. Jones, Bradley, and Jocelyn Kiley. "More 'Warmth' for Trump among GOP Voters Concerned by Immigrants, Diversity," *Pew Centre Research*, June 2, 2016, accessed June 24, 2016, http://www.pewresearch.org/fact-tank/2016/06/02/more-warmth-for-trump-among-gop-voters-concerned-by-immigrants-diversity/
50. Pew Research Center "Public Uncertain, Divided Over American's Place in the World."
51. Vinograd, Cassandra. "Donald Trump, Hilary Clinton Respond to Istanbul Airport Attack," *NBC NEWS*, June 29, 2016, accessed June 30, 2016, http://www.nbcnews.com/storyline/istanbul-ataturk-airport-attack/donald-trump-hillary-clinton-respond-istanbul-airport-attack-n600911
52. Vitali, Ali. "Donald Trump on Terror: You Have to 'Fight Fire with Fire,'" *NBC News*, June 29, 2016, accessed June 30, 2016, http://www.nbcnews.com/politics/2016-election/donald-trump-terror-you-have-fight-fire-fire-n600771
53. Vinograd. "Donald Trump, Hilary Clinton Respond to Istanbul Airport Attack."
54. Vitali. "Donald Trump on Terror."
55. Roach, David. "GOP Debate: Trump's Character Draws Focus," *Baptist Press*, March 4, 2016, accessed June 28, 2016, http://bpnews.net/46439/gop-debate-trumps-character-draws-focus
56. Hulsey. "Donald Trump Speaks to Thousands at Dayton Airport."
57. Kropf, Schuyler. "Donald Trump Drops Dime on Lindsey Graham, Gives Out Senator's Cellphone Number," *The Post and Courier*, July 21, 2015, accessed June 23, 2016, http://www.postandcourier.com/article/20150721/PC1603/150729864/trump-gives-out-graham-x2019-s-cellphone-number-after-senator-calls-him-a-x2018-jackass-x2019
58. Trump, "Donald J. Trump Foreign Policy Speech."
59. Pew Research Center "Public Uncertain, Divided Over American's Place in the World."

60. Slack, Donovan. "Exclusive: NRA to Run $2 Million Benghazi-Themed Ad Campaign for Trump," *USA TODAY*, June 29, 2016, accessed June 30, 2016 http://www.usatoday.com/story/news/politics/elections/2016/06/29/nra-2-million-ad-campaign-trump-benghazi/86484306/

61. Ibid.

62. Diamond, Jeremy, and Cassie Spodak. "Trump Rips GOP Rivals Who Broke Pledge: Kasich Touts Electability," *CNN*, June 30, 2016, accessed July 1, 2016, http://www.cnn.com/2016/06/29/politics/john-kasich-hillary-clinton-donald-trump/

Conclusion

Many authors have recently speculated about the dramatic changes Trump would usher in were he to occupy the Oval Office in 2017. The aim of this book, however, has not been to predict what an America with Trump at the helm would look like. Rather, this book has sought to detail how Trump is already influencing the country. This ongoing and incremental transformation is not only affecting American cultural and political life but also reshaping the essential meaning of the modern American national identity.

Trump's campaign has revealed that there exists a profound sense of dissatisfaction among the American public regarding how the government and the leaderships of both parties have handled issues concerning the slow economic recovery, the increased globalization and deindustrialization, the growing gap between the rich and poor, rising illegal immigration, and the escalating threat of terrorism. Trump has empowered a large cross section of the electorate whose resentment has long been suppressed because of such labels as "uneducated" and "bigot." He has helped them to find their voice by providing a space where they can openly express their grievances. He has successfully tapped into and echoed the feeling shared by large segments of the American population that the country, with its permeable borders—particularly to the south—is weak and vulnerable. He has supported their nostalgia for the past: of a strong America with a world-class workforce, assimilated citizenry, and secure national boundaries. He has echoed their desire to see the national interest of the U.S. firmly back at the top of the government agenda, in addition to a clearly defined conceptualization of American citizenship. "We've opened up a very big discussion that needed to be opened up," Trump noted at one of the GOP debates during the primaries.[1]

At the same time, by supporting and reinforcing attitudes of nationalism, Trump has created and defined clear patterns of inclusion and exclusion. In rejecting the idea of political correctness, perceived as a cover for ineffective politicians, he has justified the open expression of the disenfranchised even where it was based on prejudice and bigotry. "Today, Trump supporters voice opinions that yesterday they may have been unsure of or publically afraid to acknowledge for fear of being alone and called a 'racist' or 'bigot.'"[2] The expressions of suppressed frustration Trump has brought into the public arena have trickled down and acquired a life of its own among portions of the American population.

Once vocalized and repeated through various mass media outlets, these views have not faded. "Trump may be the icon of the movement he's ignited, but it's gone far beyond his actions or control."[3] The open expressions of prejudices have been justified and promoted by the Trump campaign to the point where they are becoming an inevitable part of the American social life. His insults and bullying, his open expressions of exclusion and aggression, coercion and dominance, have incited a sense of fierceness among both his supporters and opponents. Both sides have resorted to violence during his rallies.[4] Families are engaging in heated discussions over their support for one candidate or another, and some people have even experienced harassment because they do not like the candidate their friends support.[5]

Trump's style of social engagement has not only resonated with older generations, but the use of aggression in public has also become more acceptable among children. When the basketball team from a predominately White high school in Indiana lost to a team from a predominately Hispanic high school, the students from Indiana invoked Trump's name and statements about building the wall to keep out illegal immigrants from Mexico, as a means to harass their Hispanic rivals.[6] Schoolchildren are engaging in more bullying behavior toward minorities, refugees, and pupils from low-income and poor families, provoking anxiety among immigrants, Muslims, and other minorities. More specifically, students are displaying more aggression, in the form of name-calling, harassment, and intimidation, toward students whose races, religions, or nationalities have been the verbal targets of Trump's campaign.[7]

The rise of Trump, as a phenomenon, has also pointed to the vulnerabilities of democracy with majoritarian rule. Every country has large segments of their respective populations whose voices, steeped in dissatisfaction, are not heard and their grievances not addressed. The populist leaders such as Donald Trump have the possibility of rising up and opening the way for these groups to express their frustrations. Economic deprivation always results in scapegoating and discrimination toward the outgroups, especially toward the most vulnerable and disempowered groups in society. The movement's expansion further alienates the American public from the opinions and visions of the elites who promote the ideas of globalization, open borders, and multiculturalism. The movement reflects resentment and cultural stress, which results in a retreat toward primordial nationalistic sentiments, coercion, and exclusion. Authoritarian leaders who connect the popularity of Trump to the flaws of democratic systems have begun to emphasize this vulnerability more openly.

The popularity of Trump has demonstrated it is not only important to promote education toward tolerance and mutual co-existence but it is crucial to address issues of deindustrialization, job outsourcing, poverty and inequality, and low upward mobility. America is a land of equal opportunity and freedom, where the "American Dream" was and must be obtainable again for every one of its citizens.

Notes

1. Campbell, Troy. "Yes, Trump and Sanders Are Actually Changing America," *Politico*, January 04, 2016, accessed March 23, 2016, http://www.politico.com/magazine/story/2016/01/donald-trump-bernie-sanders-2016-changing-america-213503#ixzz4DklXNWOu
2. Ibid.
3. Heer, Jeet. "Republic of Fear," *New Republic*, March 31, 2016, accessed June 26, 2016, https://newrepublic.com/article/132114/republic-fear
4. Watch: Young Protesters Greet Trump Supporters With Hostility, Breitbart TV. May 2, 2016, accessed May 19, 2016, http://www.breitbart.com/video/2016/05/02/watch-young-protesters-greet-trump-supporters-with-hostility/;   Mathis-Lilley, Ben. "A Continually Growing List of Violent Incidents at Trump Events." *The Slatest*, April 25, 2016, accessed May 3, 2016, http://www.slate.com/blogs/the_slatest/2016/03/02/a_list_of_violent_incidents_at_donald_trump_rallies_and_events.html; Sullivan, Sean and Michael E. Miller. "Ugly, bloody scenes in San Jose as protesters attack Trump supporters outside rally." *The Washington Post*, June 3, 2016, accessed June 3, 2016, https://www.washingtonpost.com/news/morning-mix/wp/2016/06/03/ugly-bloody-scenes-in-san-jose-as-protesters-attack-trump-supporters-outside-rally/
5. BBC Staff. "The Trump Effect: Young Republicans Weigh In," *BBC*, May 16, 2016, accessed June 3, 2016, http://www.bbc.com/news/election-us-2016-36291757
6. Cuevas, Mayra. "'Trump' as Anti-Latino Epithet: Ugly Incidents at High School Games," *CNN*, March 1, 2016, accessed June 20, 2016, http://www.cnn.com/2016/03/01/us/midwest-trump-school-chants/
7. SPLC Staff. "The Trump Effect: The Impact of the Presidential Campaign on Our Nation's School," *Southern Poverty Law Center*, April 13, 2016, accessed April 13, 2016, https://www.splcenter.org/20160413/trump-effect-impact-presidential-campaign-our-nations-schools

Selected Bibliography

Alexander, Jeffrey C. "Citizen and Enemy as Symbolic Classification: On the Polarizing Discourse of Civil Society," in *Cultivating Differences: Symbolic Boundaries and the Making of Inequality*, ed. M. Fournier and M. Lamont. Chicago: Chicago University Press, (1992): 289–308.

Alexander, Jeffrey C. *The Meanings of Social Life: A Cultural Sociology*. Oxford: Oxford University Press, 2003.

Alinsky, Saul. *Rules for Radicals*. New York: Random House, (1971): 134.

Allen, Amy. *The Power of Feminist Theory: Domination, Resistance, Solidarity*, Westview Press, 1999.

Anderson, C. A., and Brad J. Bushman. "Human aggression." *Annual Review of Psychology* 53, no. 1, (2002): 27–51.

Arendt, Hannah. *The Human Condition*. Chicago: University of Chicago Press, 1958.

Arendt, Hannah. *On Violence*. New York: Harcourt, Brace & World, 1970.

Avruch, Kevin. *Context and Pretext in Conflict Resolution: Culture, Identity, Power, and Practice*. Routledge, 2015.

Barnett, Michael N., and Raymond Duvall, *Power in Global Governance*. Cambridge, UK, New York: Cambridge University Press, 2005.

Baron, Robert A., and Deborah R. Richardson. *Human Aggression*. 2nd ed. New York and London: Plenum Press, 2004.

Barth, Fredrik. *Process and Form in Social Life*. London: Routledge and Kegan Paul, 1981.

Bataille, Georges. *Literature and Evil, trans. Alastair Hamilton*. 1st ed. Marion Boyars Publishers Ltd., 2001.

Benhabib, Seyla. *The Reluctant Modernism of Hannah Arendt*. Rowman & Littlefield Publishers, 2003.

Berger, Charles R., and James J. Bradac. *Language and Social Knowledge: Uncertainty in Interpersonal Relations*. London: Arnold, 1982.

Boulding, Kenneth E. *Three Faces of Power*, Newbury Park: Sage Publications, Inc., 1990.

Bourdieu, Pierre. *Outline of a Theory of Practice*. Cambridge Studies in Social Anthropology 16. Cambridge, New York: Cambridge University Press, 1977.

Bush, Melanie. *Breaking the Code of Good Intention: Everyday Forms of Whiteness*. New York: Rowman & Littlefield, 2005.

Cartwright, Dorwin. *Studies in Social Power.* Research Center for Group Dynamics, Institute for Social Research, University of Michigan, 1959.

Cohen, Anthony P. *The Symbolic Construction of Community.* London: Tavistock, 1985.

Davis, J. A. "A Formal Interpretation of the Theory of Relative Deprivation." *Sociometry* 22, (1959): 280–296.

Devos, Thierry, and Mahzarin R. Banaji. "American = White?" *Journal of Personality and Social Psychology* 88, (2005): 447–466.

Festinger, Leon. *A Theory of Cognitive Dissonance.* Stanford, CA: Stanford University Press, 1957.

Foucault, Michel. *The History of Sexuality.* Harmondsworth: Penguin Books, 1981.

French, John R. P., and Bertram. Raven. "The Bases of Social Power," in *Studies in Social Power*, ed. Dorwin Cartwright. Research Center for Group Dynamics, Institute for Social Research, University of Michigan, (1959): 150–167.

Gellner, Ernest. *Nations and Nationalism (New Perspectives on the Past) [Paperback].* Ithaca, NY: Cornell University Press, 1983.

Gergen, Kenneth J. *The Saturated Self, Dilemmas of Identity in Contemporary Life.* 2nd ed. New York: Basic Books, 2001.

Goffman, Erving. *Frame Analysis: An Essay on the Organization of Experience.* Harper & Row, 1974.

Groom, A. J. R., and K. Webb. "Injustice, Empowerment and Facilitation in Conflict." *International Interactions* 13, no. 3, (1987): 263–280.

Gurr, Ted R. *Minorities at Risk. A Global View of Ethnopolitical Conflict.* Washington, DC: United States Institute of Peace, 1993.

Habermas, Jurgen. "Citizenship and National Identity," in *Between Facts and Norms: Contributions to a Discourse Theory of Law and Democracy.* Cambridge: MIT Press, 1998.

Hammack, Phillip L. *Narrative and the Politics of Identity: The Cultural Psychology of Israeli and Palestinian Youth.* 1st ed. Oxford, USA: Oxford University Press, 2010.

Harré, Rom, and Luk Van Langenhove, eds. *Positioning Theory: Moral Contexts of International Action.* 1st ed. Wiley-Blackwell, (1998): 5–347.

Horowitz, Donald L. "Ethnic Identity," in *Ethnicity, theory and experience*, eds. N. Glazer, and D. Moynihan. Cambridge: Harvard University Press, 1975.

Huntington, Samuel. *Who Are We?: The Challenges to American's National Identity.* New York, NY: Simon & Schuster, 2004.

Hutnik, Nimmi. *Ethnic Minority Identity.* Oxford: Clarendon Press, 1991.

Isenberg, Nancy. *White Trash: The 400-Year Untold History of Class in America.* Penguin, 2016.

Kelman, Herbert. "Reflections on the Social and Pyschological Processes of Legitimization and Delegitimization," in *The Psychology of Legitimacy: Emergin Perspectives on Ideology, Justice, and Intergroup Relations*, ed. J. T. Jost and B. Major, Cambridge University Press, (2001): 54–73.

Korostelina, Karina V. *Political Insults: How Offenses Escalate Conflict.* Oxford: Oxford University Press, 2014.

Leonardelli, G. J., and Marilynn B. Brewer. "Minority and Majority Discrimination: When and Why?" in *Journal of Experimental Social Psychology* 37, (2001): 468–485.

Moghaddam, Fathali M. "The Psychological Citizen and the Two Concepts of Social Contract: A Preliminary Analysis." *Political Psychology* 29, no. 6, (2008): 881–901.

Moscovici, Serge. *Social Influence and Social Change.* Published in cooperation with European Association of Experimental Social Psychology by Academic Press, 1976.

Milgram, Stanley. *Obedience to Authority: An Experimental View.* Harpercollins, 1974.

Otten, Sabin, Amelie Mummendey, and Mathias Blanz. "Intergroup Discrimination in Positive and Negative Outcome Allocations: Impact of Stimulus Valence, Relative Group Status, and Relative Group Size." *Personality and Social Psychology Bulletin* 22, (1996): 567–581.

Packer, George. *The Unwinding: An Inner History of the New America.* Macmillan, 2013.Parsons, Talcott. *Essays in Sociological Theory.* Glencoe, Ill: Free Press, (1954): 126.

Rothbart, Daniel, and Karina V. Korostelina, eds. *Identity, Morality, and Threat: Studies in Violent Conflict.* Lexington, MA: Lexington Books, 2006.

Rothbart, Daniel, and Karina V. Korostelina. *Why They Die: Civilian Devastation in Violent Conflict.* University of Michigan Press, 2011.

Runciman, Walter Garrison. *Relative Deprivation and Social Justice: A Study of Attitudes to Social Inequality in Twentieth Century England.* Berkeley: University of California Press, 1966.

Sharp, Gene. *The Politics of Nonviolent Action.* Boston: P. Sargent Publisher, 1973.

Somin, Ilya. *Democracy and Political Ignorance: Why Smaller Government Is Smarter.* Standford, CA: Stanford University Press, 2013.

Tajfel, Henri, ed. *Differentiation between Social Groups: Studies in the Social Psychology of Intergroup Relations.* Academic Press, 1979.

Tajfel, Henri, and John C. Turner. "The Social Identity Theory of Intergroup Behaviour," in *Psychology of Intergroup Relations*, ed. Stephen Worchel and William G. Austin, 2nd ed. Chicago: Nelson-Hall, (1985): 7–24.

Tanter, Raymond, and Ted R. Gurr. "Why Men Rebel." *Midwest Journal of Political Science* 14, no. 4, (1970): 725.

Tilly, Charles. *The Politics of Collective Violence.* Cambridge: Cambridge University Press, 2003.

Tilly, Charles. *Identities, Boundaries and Social Ties.* Boulder: Paradigm, 2005.

Tilly, Charles. *Regimes and Repertoires.* Chicago: University of Chicago Press, 2006.

Tiryakian, Edward A. "Collective Effervescence, Social Change and Charism: Durkheim, Weber and 1989." *International Sociology* 10, no. 3, (1995): 269–281.

Turner, John C., M. A. Hogg, P. J., Oakes, S. D. Reicher, & M. S. Wetherell. *Rediscovering the Social Group: A Self-Categorization Theory*, Cambridge, MA: Basil Blackwel, (1987): 50.

Sugrue, Thomas J. *The Origins of the Urban Crisis: Race and Inequality in Postwar Detroit.* Princeton: Princeton University Press, 1996.

Weber, Max. *Economy and Society: An Outline of Interpretive Sociology.* University of California Press, 1978.

Weiner, Bernard. *An Attributional Theory of Motivation and Emotion.* New York: Springer-Verlag, 1986.

Index

For Product Safety Concerns and Information please contact our EU
representative GPSR@taylorandfrancis.com
Taylor & Francis Verlag GmbH, Kaufingerstraße 24, 80331 München, Germany